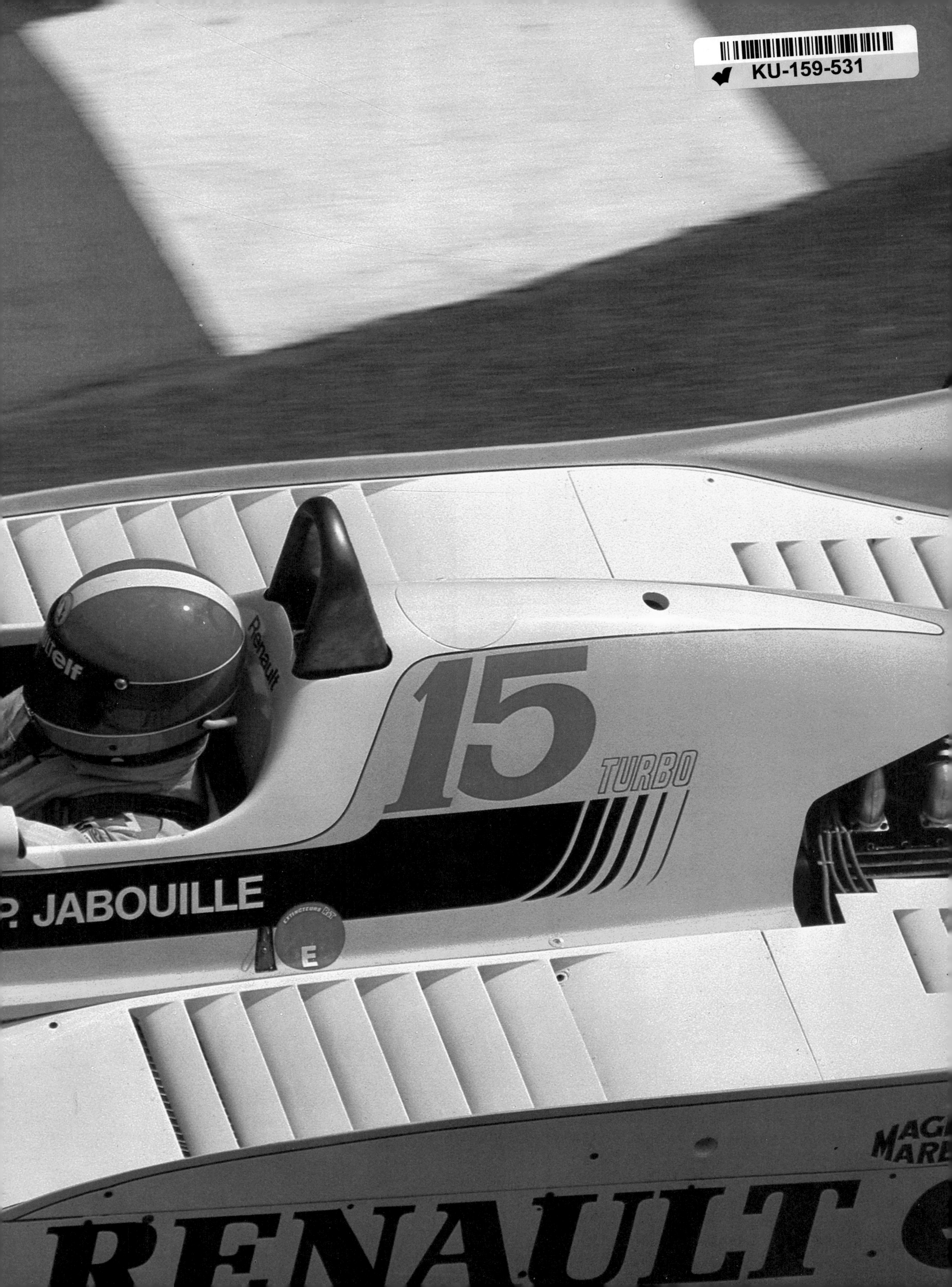
Renault
15
TURBO
P. JABOUILLE
E
RENAULT

MOTOR SPORTS

MOTOR SPORTS

Jeffrey Daniels

Sundial

Contents

Endpaper photograph Jean-Pierre Jabouille in the Renault turbocharged Formula 1 car

Half-title page photograph Foresti (Ballot) in the 1922 Targa Florio

Title-page photograph Jody Scheckter in the 1979 Formula 1 Ferrari

Contents-page photograph Greg Carr and Fred Gocentas (Ford Escort RS) in the 1979 RAC Rally

First published in Great Britain in 1980 by
Sundial Publications Limited
59 Grosvenor Street London W1

© 1980 Hennerwood Publications Limited

ISBN 0 906320 06 2

Produced by Mandarin Publishers Limited
22a Westlands Road Quarry Bay Hong Kong

Printed in Hong Kong

Le Petit Journal

SUPPLÉMENT ILLUSTRÉ

Huit pages : CINQ centimes

TOUS LES JOURS
Le Petit Journal
5 Centimes

TOUS LES DIMANCHES
Le Supplément illustré
5 Centimes

Cinquième année | LUNDI 6 AOUT 1894 | Numéro 194

Concours du « Petit Journal »

LES VOITURES SANS CHEVAUX

Origins

Man has always had an urge to race, and it was only a few years after the world's first motor cars had puttered tentatively along public roads in the 1880s that intrepid 'automobilists' began to organise a whole range of competitions. The earliest cars were notoriously unreliable, and many informal contests held in those days consisted of several cars setting off from a starting point, with victory going to the last one to suffer mechanical breakdown. The first formal reliability trial was organised by a French magazine in 1894 and was run from Paris to Rouen, a distance of 127km (79 miles). More than 20 cars took part, including a couple of De Dion-Bouton steam-powered delivery vans, and all but four completed the course.

Soon genuine races, in which high speed and driving skill were as important as reliability, became popular. The first major long-distance road race, from Paris to Bordeaux and back, was in 1895; the first hill-climb race, from Nice to La Turbie (in the mountains above Monaco), was in 1897; and the first sprint meeting, held at Achères (near Paris), was in 1898. Note that all these events took place in France: although the Germans Karl Benz and Gottlieb Daimler had produced the first practical petrol-engined cars, it was in France that motoring fever first took hold and where the motor industry was born; and it was French motoring organisations – notably the Automobile Club de France (ACF) and the various regional clubs – that organised many of the first major sporting events and developed the ground rules on which international racing was to be based.

Paris became the starting point for a series of inter-city races, notably to Marseilles (1896), Berlin (1901), Vienna (1902), and Madrid (1903). This last race, in which many of the cars were capable of 145km/h (90mph) or more, ended in tragedy: two drivers, three riding mechanics, and a number of spectators (probably half a million lined the route) were killed in a series of accidents on the first leg. The event was stopped at Bordeaux. Henceforward out-and-out racing would (with a few important exceptions) be confined to private circuits or public roads temporarily closed to normal traffic.

The origins of *grand-prix* racing lie not so much in those inter-city events as in the Gordon Bennett Cup, which on occasion was run concurrently with them. The event took its name from its sponsor, an expatriate American newspaper magnate. It differed from other races in that entrants consisted of national teams – each country being allowed to enter a team of three cars built by native manufacturers. For the first two years of its brief life the cup race was a bit of a farce: in 1900 only five cars competed, three from France and one each from the United States and Belgium; in 1901 a French team were the only starters. The following year, when the Gordon Bennett was combined with the Paris–Vienna marathon, a British two-car team carried off the cup, the individual winner being S. F. Edge in a 6.5-litre, 30hp Napier.

Edge's victory gave Britain the honour of org-

LEFT France was the birthplace of motor sports. This painting, on the front cover of *Le Petit Journal* of 6 August 1894, shows cars before the start of the Paris–Rouen reliability trial organised by the magazine. As cars improved, such trials gave way to inter-city races.

ABOVE, UPPER The 35PS model of 1901, designed by the great Wilhelm Maybach, was the first Daimler to bear the name Mercedes. Its advanced design created a sensation that year at Nice Race Week, where the car won most of the events in which it was entered.

ABOVE, LOWER The Gordon Bennett Cup races for national teams were forerunners of *grands prix*. The picture shows Baron de Caters in a Mercedes 60PS in the 1903 event at Athy in Ireland. The winner that year was the Belgian ace Camille Jenatzy in a similar car.

anising the 1903 event, which posed a tricky problem because road racing was banned in the United Kingdom. Eventually a closed circuit at Athy, south-west of Dublin, was found. It was the scene of one of the best of the cup races, with teams from Germany, France, and the United States as well as from Britain, and with several of the greatest drivers of the day taking part. The winning car was a 9.2-litre Mercedes 60PS – the outstanding racer of its time – driven by the Belgian 'Red Devil', Camille Jenatzy; the team prize went to France, represented by the Chevalier René de Knyff and Henri Farman in Panhards and Fernand Gabriel in a Mors.

The Gordon Bennett Cup was held in the two following years, attracting teams from many countries. But by this time France – and particularly the French motor manufacturers – had become exasperated by the regulation that limited each national entry to three cars. The exasperation was understandable, for by now there were many car makers in France building racers good enough to compete in the event; apart from Panhard and Mors and the two major firms of Renault and Peugeot, fast and powerful racers were being made by marques such as Clément-Bayard, Darracq, De Diétrich, Gobron-Brillié, Richard-Brasier, and Turcat-Méry.

The French rebelled against the restraints of the cup race, and the ACF – by now not merely the controlling motor-sport club in France but the dominant force in racing throughout Europe – decided to organise an international event that would be open to all manufacturers. Thus was born the Grand Prix de l'Automobile Club de France (which is still the official title of the French Grand Prix). It was first held in 1906: it killed the Gordon Bennett Cup stone dead, and it set a pattern that has been followed by international *grand-prix* racing ever since.

The early years of this century also saw a growing interest in time-regulated trials, and this interest found its most important early expression in the Herkomer Trophy of 1905 (the event took its name from a German-born British artist, Sir Hubert von Herkomer, who sculpted the trophy and presented it to the German Automobile Club, which organised the trial). The Herkomer was the first international event to put a premium on navigational skills and an ability to maintain high average speeds from one stage of a route to the next. The trial was to be held only twice more, one reason being that the enormous complexity of its regulations invariably led to acrimony and outraged protests by drivers who had been penalised for minor (and often obscure) technical infringements.

The Herkomer Trophy was followed in 1908 by the Prince Henry Trial (Prinz Heinrichfahrt), named after the German Kaiser's brother, a keen if not very gifted motor-sportsman. The Prince Henry Trial was at once simpler than the Herkomer and much more ambitious, its long route taking in parts of what are now Poland, Hungary, and Austria as well as Germany. It, too, lasted for only three years – possibly because in 1910 the expected victory by the 'home' team, Mercedes, was thwarted by the fast and powerful 5.7-litre, overhead-camshaft Austro-Daimlers de-

signed by the great Ferdinand Porsche (who was to work for Mercedes in the 1920s); the Austrian entry took the first three places, with Porsche himself driving the winning car, and two other Austro-Daimlers were in the first 10.

Although short-lived, the Herkomer and Prince Henry are historically important because they were the forerunners of two distinct types of classic motor sports. Their emphasis on navigation and time-keeping skills combined with various special tests finds expression today in the great international rallies; their exclusion of out-and-out racing cars in favour of 'tourers' (precursors of the sports car) foreshadowed the evolution of the great sports-car endurance races.

ABOVE Major inter-city racing in France ended with the catastrophic Paris–Madrid event of 1903. Here Fernand Gabriel awaits the start in his streamlined 11.6-litre Mors.

BELOW The Pekin–Paris marathon of 1907 was more a test of endurance than of speed. Here two De Dion-Boutons pause in Irkutsk, Siberia.

LEFT The Herkomer Trophy was the first big European event to introduce control-point checks and to put an emphasis on navigational skills – both features of the modern rally. Here Paul Nauk in a 6.9-litre Martini (the best-known Swiss marque of its day) roars away at the start of the last Herkomer in 1907.

BELOW The Prince Henry Trial, which replaced the Herkomer, was an endurance event taking in much of central Europe and attracted drivers of big and powerful touring cars. Fritz Opel (one of five brothers to found the German marque in 1898) is seen here in one of the firm's cars in the first Prince Henry of 1908.

Rallies

A rally differs from a race in that, ostensibly at least, the competitors are driving against the clock rather than against their rivals. Traditionally, rallies have put a premium on navigational skills and on the ability to keep strictly to time schedules between series of control points along the route, with drivers being penalised for lateness. This is still the basic format, but in recent years, with time schedules becoming increasingly stringent – especially on selected 'special stages' of a route – international rallies have placed far greater emphasis on sheer speed and far less on navigation. Increasingly, too, the important special stages are run not on public roads but on cross-country tracks. Such rallies, which nowadays dominate the events qualifying for the world championship, have seen the emergence of a breed of specialist drivers and of versions of car models developed solely for rallying. Once upon a time, however, things were very different – especially in what is now the sole survivor from the old days, the Monte Carlo Rally. . . .

PRECEDING TWO PAGES A
Lancia Stratos breasts a
hill in the 1976 Safari
Rally. Note the extra
spare wheel, the battery
of spotlights behind a
protective cover, and the
driver's intercom set
(used for talking to his
co-driver). The Stratos,
strong and very fast, was
one of the great rally
'specials' of the 1970s.

Monte Carlo Rally

In the early days of the Monte Carlo Rally, the word 'rally' meant exactly what it said: competitors, who were allowed to start from points all over Europe, would converge on and finally muster at Monte Carlo. The event was originally a commercial venture, intended to attract visitors to Monaco during the winter season; but it proved popular from the start. In 1911, the first year, 23 crews entered; in 1912 no fewer than 87 cars started from points as distant as Turin, Le Havre, and St Petersburg (Leningrad). The average speed required on both these occasions was 24km/h (15mph). The next Monte was in March 1924, but the following year the date was restored to January so that the weather would provide a greater challenge. Even in those days, however, drivers were arriving at Monte Carlo with few or no penalty points for lateness, so the organisers had to think of ways to find a clear winner. In 1925 they introduced a special 80km (50-mile) trial in the mountains above Monaco; in the 1930s they added a series of driving tests on the promenade at Monte Carlo.

The rally remained a preserve of the rich (if gifted) amateur driver throughout the 1920s and 1930s. Although success demanded great skill on the part of crews, the increasingly complex jumble of regulations, and the fact that local weather might give a much easier journey from one starting point than from another, discouraged car manufacturers from entering works teams: the event was too much of a lottery.

The situation changed dramatically after World War II (the first post-war Monte was in 1949). For one thing, the rally became enormously popular with the general public and began to attract several hundred entries. The press coverage of the event, and the publicity given to the successful marques and drivers, could no longer be ignored by the car makers. Moreover, the organisers largely eliminated the advantages or disadvantages of one starting point over another by arranging for all the cars to converge on a particular point (such as Paris) from which they would follow a common route on the long run down to Monaco. From the mid-1950s, then, factory teams began to appear on the scene – notably Citroën and Renault from France, Mercedes-Benz and Porsche from West Germany, and BMC, the Rootes Group, and Ford from Britain.

It must be said that the organisers have not always ingratiated themselves with either the factories or the international public. There has always been a suspicion that the French have regarded the Monte as *their* rally and that, on occasion, either the regulations or the scrutineers have unfairly favoured local cars or crews. One such occasion was the 1961 event when the 'factor of comparison' (based on engine capacity and power) was so framed as virtually to guarantee victory to the sluggish, bulbous 845cc Panhard PL17s as long as they managed to finish. They duly took first, second, and third places – and the rally's reputation took a dive.

By the early 1960s the Monte had assumed its present form. The number of starting points had been reduced, and the common route began in earnest at Chambéry (east of Lyons). From here it was a hard slog over the mountains (usually snow-covered) to Monte Carlo – but even then the rally was far from finished. Instead of the relatively easy driving tests of pre-war days there was another exhausting night of driving for the surviving cars – a loop of special stages that demanded dauntingly high speeds on icy mountain roads, where even the smallest error would be heavily penalised.

It was in these exceptionally testing circumstances that the BMC Mini gained its reputation as one of the truly great rally cars. The entry list for the 1965 event was formidable. It included the Finnish drivers Timo Mäkinen and Rauno Aaltonen and the Ulsterman Paddy Hopkirk in Mini Cooper Ss; Erik Carlsson, Pat Carlsson (Stirling Moss's sister), and Ove Andersson in Saab 96s; Eugen Böhringer (at 43 an aging but still brilliant rally driver) in a 2-litre flat-eight Porsche 904 GTS – virtually a racing car; Roger Clark in one of the new Rover 2000 saloons; Simo Lampinen in a Triumph Spitfire; and the Polish driver Sobieslaw Zasada in a Steyr-Puch, a tiny car based on the Fiat 500 but with a very lively 650cc engine. The principal French challenge came from the three works Citroën DS21s, driven by the Italian Lucien (Luciano) Bianchi, Hélène Pointet, and Hubert Marang. In all 237 cars started the rally. In those days they had not quite reached the stage of perfection for purpose of the cars of the 1970s – no two-way radios, no limitless supplies of very special tyres – but they were still far from being ordinary road cars. With engines tuned for far more power, banks of powerful extra driving lights, and interiors jammed with controls and equipment, they showed just how much effort the various manufacturers' competition workshops put into winning.

The winter of 1964/5 was dismal. As the competitors converged on Chambéry it was raining steadily, and it seemed as if it would rain for ever. Already 26 cars had retired. At Chambéry itself the rain turned to snow. Far to the south, beyond

BELOW The winner of the
first Monte Carlo Rally in
1911 – Henri Rougier's
stately Turcat-Méry. Of
23 cars to enter that
year, 16 managed to
reach the finish.

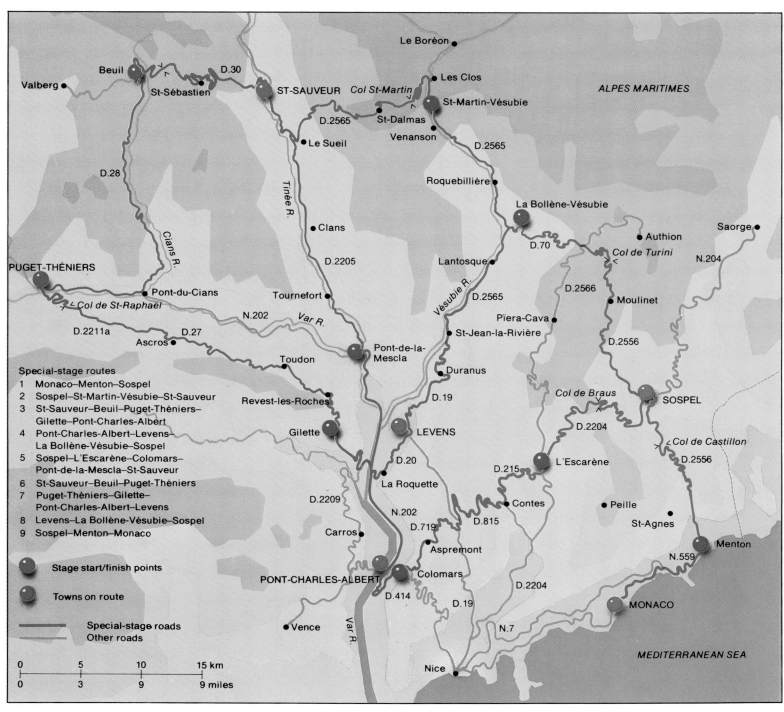

Map labels (for reference within the figure):

Le Boréon · Valberg · Beuil · St-Sébastien · D.30 · ST-SAUVEUR · Les Clos · Col St-Martin · St-Martin-Vésubie · ALPES MARITIMES · D.2565 · St-Dalmas · Venanson · D.28 · Le Sueil · Tinée R. · Roquebillière · D.2565 · La Bollène-Vésubie · Cians R. · Clans · Authion · Saorge · PUGET-THÉNIERS · D.2205 · Lantosque · Col de Turini · N.204 · Pont-du-Cians · D.70 · Col de St-Raphaël · Tournefort · D.2566 · Moulinet · Vésubie R. · D.2565 · N.202 · Var R. · Piera-Cava · D.2211a · D.27 · St-Jean-la-Rivière · D.2556 · Ascros · Toudon · Pont-de-la-Mescla · Duranus · Col de Braus · D.19 · Revest-les-Roches · SOSPEL · Gilette · LEVENS · Col de Castillon · D.2204 · D.2556 · D.20 · D.215 · L'Escarène · La Roquette · D.2209 · N.202 · Contes · Peille · Carros · D.719 · D.815 · St-Agnes · Aspremont · Menton · PONT-CHARLES-ALBERT · Colomars · D.2204 · N.559 · D.414 · D.19 · MONACO · Vence · Var R. · N.7 · Nice · MEDITERRANEAN SEA

Special-stage routes
1 Monaco–Menton–Sospel
2 Sospel–St-Martin-Vésubie–St-Sauveur
3 St-Sauveur–Beuil–Puget-Théniers–
   Gilette–Pont-Charles-Albert
4 Pont-Charles-Albert–Levens–
   La Bollène-Vésubie–Sospel
5 Sospel–L'Escarène–Colomars–
   Pont-de-la-Mescla–St-Sauveur
6 St-Sauveur–Beuil–Puget-Théniers
7 Puget-Théniers–Gilette–
   Pont-Charles-Albert–Levens
8 Levens–La Bollène-Vésubie–Sospel
9 Sospel–Menton–Monaco

 Stage start/finish points

 Towns on route

— Special-stage roads
— Other roads

0   5   10   15 km
0   3   9   9 miles

the mountains, it was raining in Monte Carlo as well – a sure sign of bad conditions in the mountains. Bad they certainly were.

In theory, snow and ice no longer held terrors for the top rally drivers. Studded tyres had made an enormous difference to adhesion in such conditions, often allowing the best drivers to brake, corner, and accelerate away almost as if they were on a dry road. But in 1965 it was a different story. From Chambéry 211 of the greatest rally drivers in the world set off southwards into the night and the mountains; only 35 arrived at Monte Carlo – and most of them had accumulated too many penalty points to stand any chance of winning. The route between Chambéry and Grenoble was a single special stage of 47km (29 miles) taking in the famous Col du Granier and the difficult Col du Cucheron. It was a white hell all the way – the snow turned to a blizzard driven by gale-force winds.

At rally speeds these are not nice roads to drive. One's powerful lights seem to spend half their time looking at a towering rock face, and the other half staring out over the edge of the road into the empty abyss beyond. On this night in 1965 the drivers were lucky to see that much; the thick snowflakes driven against the screen were worse than any fog, while even the studded tyres often scrabbled vainly for a grip in the fresh, dry, powdery surface. One by one, all but a handful of the most-fancied teams dropped out.

The surviving cars groped their way through the centre of Grenoble, and plunged into the blizzard once more, to the next special stage over the Col de Chamrousse and down the minor roads towards Gap. Here the snow was not quite so bad – it was merely falling steadily instead of creating the 'white-out' effect of earlier hours. By now the BMC team was reduced to two Minis: Aaltonen had

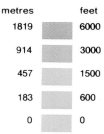

metres		feet
1819		6000
914		3000
457		1500
183		600
0		0

Map of the nine special speed stages at the end of the 1965 Monte Carlo Rally. The highest point on the routes is the Col de Turini at 1,607m (5,272ft).

13

Paddy Hopkirk (Mini Cooper) approaches the final control point on his way to victory in the 1964 Monte Carlo Rally. The agile Minis were a dominant force in European rallies in the early and mid-1960s.

not crashed or got irretrievably embedded in a snowdrift, as had already happened to many other drivers. He was halted, believe it or not, by a condenser coming adrift and jamming the distributor mechanism – and the damage was too great to permit roadside repairs.

Beyond Gap lay the Saint Apollinaire special stage, and here a second near-disaster hit the Minis. Hopkirk's car slid off the road and hit a rock, tearing one of the front suspension wishbones clear of its mounting. Hopkirk and his co-driver Henry Liddon dragged the car back onto the road and carried on – with the front (driving) wheels pointing in quite different directions – until they reached their service point, where the wishbone was hastily, crudely welded back into place. But they, too, had lost precious minutes.

The service points were like something out of a nightmare. Cars would appear, lights blazing, engines roaring, to pick their way past the huddle of vans and people, their drivers looking for the sign that indicated their own crew. The mechanics worked feverishly in the gale-driven snow under a blaze of arc lights, the cold eating at their fingers as they struggled to replace brake pads, change wheels, check engines. Everything had to be done with the utmost speed: a car might have ten minutes for repairs and a major check before it was due at the next time control. But even that was better than it was for the service crews waiting for cars which never appeared. Some had suffered mechanical failure; some had crashed; some crews, with nerves and eyes no longer equal to the strain and with their lateness allowance running out, had given up the struggle, pulled clear of the road, and gone to sleep.

When the cars reached Monaco it was clear that the run from Chambéry had been the most terrible

ABOVE The Citroën DS21s, with front-wheel drive, were the most formidable big saloons in the Monte during the 1960s. Here Hélène Pointet, one of the best women rally drivers of her day, takes her DS21 over the Col des Leques during the 1966 event, which was won by her Finnish team-mate Pauli Toivonen after the 'winning' Minis had been disqualified for allegedly faulty lighting.

RIGHT Front-wheel drive again: this one is a Lancia Fulvia coupé negotiating an ice-bound right-hander on the Col de Turini in 1969. At that time the nippy Fulvia's narrow-V4 engine was of 1.3 litres. Later it was bored out to 1.6 litres and, in the hands of Sandro Munari, won the 1972 Monte.

in the history of the rally. All the team managers and almost all the drivers had near-catastrophes to report. There was one exception to this catalogue of woe: Timo Mäkinen had not only been easily the quickest driver over the whole series of special stages; almost unbelievably, he had not suffered a single penalty point for lateness at any of the control points. Hopkirk's troubles in the other Mini had dropped him to 18th place; Mäkinen's chief threat lay in two of the works Citroëns, which lay second and third and were expected to do well in the special speed stages above Monaco on the following night. There were nine special stages, most of them over serpentine minor roads that took the competitors over formidable passes, including the famous Col de Turini with its series of ice-bound hairpin bends. Most of the experts assumed that the leading French drivers, who were more familiar with the terrain and were driving cars more powerful than Mäkinen's, would have a decisive advantage –

assuming that the roads were fit for driving at all.

It did not work out like that. Mäkinen never put a wheel wrong: it was the Citroën team that came to grief. Bianchi hit a tree, Hélène Pointet suffered brake failure, and Marang crashed down a steep bank (his co-driver was seriously injured). With its front-runners gone, Citroën stood no hope. Instead, it was left to Böhringer's racing Porsche and Pat Carlsson's Saab to chase the Mini home and gain second and third places. Peter Harper brought the powerful Sunbeam Tiger home in fourth place, and Roger Clark came sixth in the Rover 2000. It had been an astonishing rally in which the weather had played the most important part. All that could be said about the crews who finished is that, apart from their driving ability, they had shown themselves to be fit, brave, and determined. As for the Mini Cooper S, it had proved to any who still doubted it that front-wheel drive was a tremendous advantage on snow and ice, and that the small car needed no 'factor of

BELOW In recent years the Monte has been dominated by powerful sports cars, notably the Porsche 911 and the Ferrari-engined Lancia Stratos – both rear engined and with rear-wheel drive. Here Jean-Pierre Nicolas corners in a 911 Turbo in the snow-mantled Alpes Maritimes during the 1978 event.

comparison' to protect it against more powerful, but less nimble, machinery. It had, indeed, won in 1964 (Paddy Hopkirk, starting from Minsk in the Soviet Union); it would have won in 1966 but for a dubious quibble regarding its lighting system; it won for the third time in 1967 in the hands of Rauno Aaltonen; and its victories in other important rallies during this period were legion.

Those were the great days of the Monte. Today the magic of its name remains for the general public, but it no longer attracts the massive and enthusiastic entries of former years. It is now essentially a competition between expensively prepared works teams, who can afford to deploy dozens of service vehicles and mechanics and hundreds of special tyres, not to mention half a dozen reconnaissance cars whose job is to chart the ice conditions on the special stages almost up to the moment they start. The romance has gone out of the Monte, but at least it survives – which is more than can be said for the Alpine Rally.

ABOVE Monte traffic jam: a Fiat 131 Abarth, stuck in the mountains, is passed by two others and a Lancia Stratos during the run down to Monte Carlo in 1978. The Abarth, a specially developed version of the Fiat 131 saloon, has proved a formidable rival to the Ford Escort RS in European rallies during the 1970s.

LEFT Spectators lining the tortuous Alpine route in the 1979 Monte heave Jean Ragnotti's Renault 5 out of a snowdrift.

The Coupe des Alpes

In the years between the two world wars, the Austrian Alpine Trial (first run in 1910) was almost the only great rally apart from the Monte. In many ways it was held in even higher esteem: a tour of many of the stiffest Alpine passes, it was a real test of car and driver; it was held in the summer so that the lottery aspect of snow- or ice-bound roads was absent. Its popularity was such that it gradually evolved into an international event taking in not only Austria but Italy, Switzerland, France, and Germany. Unlike the Monte, its more serious and less chancy nature attracted the works teams; and to give every type of manufacturer a sporting chance it was divided into five classes depending on engine capacities. One of its unique features was that in theory there was no winner: anybody who emerged with no 'demerits' (penalty points) won a Coupe des Glaciers, while for the team with fewest demerits there was the manufacturers' team prize. The attraction of the Alpine was that, given the schedules set and the road conditions in the high passes, it was only a superb (if at times lucky) combination of car and driver that could lay claim to a *coupe*.

It became almost a matter of pride to the organisers that their time schedules should be so well calculated as to result in no more than a handful of awards, and preferably only one. Their neatest calculation of pre-war years came in 1933 when only three individuals earned themselves clean sheets out of a total entry of 132 cars. There was a strong field that year, with works-sponsored teams of three from Ford (entered from Holland, and running in the unlimited class), Hotchkiss, Mercedes-Benz, Adler, Vauxhall, Riley, Frazer Nash, MG, Singer, and Fiat.

The rally started from Merano in the South Tyrol (now the Alto Adige) and took in Vipiteno and Cortina d'Ampezzo (on the first day), Gomagoi, Pontresina, and St Moritz (second day), Lugano, Varese, and Turin (third day), Briançon and Grenoble (fourth day), and Gap, Embrun, and finally Nice (fifth day). The routes linking these towns, of course, took in the most formidable mountain roads and passes the organisers could

The Austrian Alpine Trial was the outstanding international rally of the inter-war years, calling for great driving skill as well as for efficient navigation and time-keeping. The pictures on this page show the kinds of mountain roads the drivers had to contend with in the 1920s. Three- or even four-man crews were the norm; the cars were generally 'tourers' – open four-seaters.

ABOVE An Itala Tipo 515 in the Italian Alps.

BELOW A four-cylinder, 3.5-litre Nazzaro gets a push at a check point.

find. Many of these passes – such as the Stelvio, Bernina, Fluela, and Julier – can today be negotiated by the average driver with little difficulty. In 1933, however, things were quite different: the roads were narrower, the corners were sharper, the gradients were steeper, the surfaces were rougher (a mixture of gravel and dirt), and the edges of precipitous drops were unprotected by posts or barriers. Yet the rally drivers had to tackle them at high speed – and put their trust in brake systems that were markedly inferior to those of today.

The rally proved a formidable test from the very start, and the organisers must have been delighted with the relentless accumulation of demerits: only 30 drivers remained unpenalised after the first day, and only seven after the second day. Still to come was a series of daunting French passes, notably the Col de l'Izoard (even today one of the most difficult passes in the Alps) and the very high Col du Galibier.

From that point on, the Alpine route was remarkably similar to that of the 1965 Monte Carlo Rally, although it was high summer and there was no chance of encountering a blizzard. There was a stop at Grenoble, and on the last day the route passed on through Gap. Major Anthony Lago (who in 1936 was to take over the ailing firm of Talbot, and produced the sports-racing Lago-Talbots) lost a rear wheel on the Col Bayard. Displaying the indefatigable approach of those days, he recovered it, filed and chiselled the hub until the wheel would fit again, and carried on.

Such heroics were in vain. At the end of the rally only three drivers remained unpenalised: Walter Delmar in a Bugatti Type 43GT (a supercharged 2.3-litre tourer); René Carrière in an Alfa Romeo 6C-1750 (a supercharged two-seater); and H.J. Aldington in a 1.5-litre, chain-driven Frazer Nash. The team prize went to the three Hotchkiss AM80 3-litre tourers, which acquired only 36 demerit points between them; next best was the Riley Imp team, with 51 points.

After World War II the Alpine was revived by

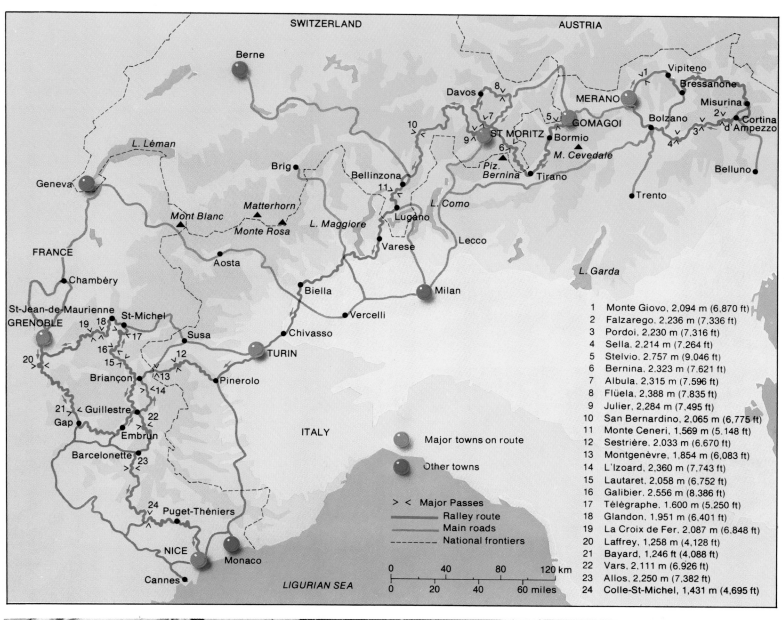

1	Monte Giovo,	2,094 m (6,870 ft)
2	Falzarego,	2,236 m (7,336 ft)
3	Pordoi,	2,230 m (7,316 ft)
4	Sella,	2,214 m (7,264 ft)
5	Stelvio,	2,757 m (9,046 ft)
6	Bernina,	2,323 m (7,621 ft)
7	Albula,	2,315 m (7,596 ft)
8	Flüela,	2,388 m (7,835 ft)
9	Julier,	2,284 m (7,495 ft)
10	San Bernardino,	2,065 m (6,775 ft)
11	Monte Ceneri,	1,569 m (5.148 ft)
12	Sestrière,	2,033 m (6,670 ft)
13	Montgenèvre,	1,854 m (6,083 ft)
14	L'Izoard,	2,360 m (7,743 ft)
15	Lautaret,	2,058 m (6,752 ft)
16	Galibier,	2,556 m (8,386 ft)
17	Télégraphe,	1.600 m (5,250 ft)
18	Glandon,	1,951 m (6,401 ft)
19	La Croix de Fer,	2,087 m (6,848 ft)
20	Laffrey,	1,258 m (4,128 ft)
21	Bayard,	1,246 ft (4,088 ft)
22	Vars,	2,111 m (6,926 ft)
23	Allos,	2,250 m (7,382 ft)
24	Colle-St-Michel,	1,431 m (4,695 ft)

Major towns on route

Other towns

> < Major Passes

———— Ralley route

———— Main roads

– – – – National frontiers

0   40   80   120 km
0 20 40 60 miles

ABOVE Map of the 1933 Alpine Trial, which proved to be one of the most difficult of the 1930s – only three of the cars arriving at Nice with no penalty points.

LEFT One of the penalty-free cars in 1933 was the 1.5-litre Frazer Nash of H.J. Aldington, seen here (behind the wheel of car number 86) with others of the Frazer Nash team that year. Aldington, who had bought the firm of Frazer Nash in 1929, also achieved penalty-free runs in 1932 and 1934.

ABOVE The informality of pre-war rallies is evident in this scene at Nice before the start of the 1934 Alpine. The front row includes three sporty little Singer Nines, which did well in the trials of that era.

LEFT One of the most formidable passes to feature in the Alpine was the Stelvio (on the Swiss/Italian frontier north-east of Bormio), which climbs to 2,757m (9,045ft). Part of the dizzying series of hairpin bends on the Italian side can be seen on the right in the photograph.

the French, and henceforward was known formally as the Coupe des Alpes. One of the greatest years was in 1952, when the rally started at Marseilles and included overnight stops at Cortina d'Ampezzo, Menaggio, and Aix-les-Bains (north of Chambéry), and finished at Cannes. The expansion of tourism in the Alpine region had by now enforced the improvement of roads over many of the high passes; but, by the same token, the drivers had to cope with a much greater density of traffic, including coaches and lorries, on many stretches of the route. Near Cortina the drivers had to face the additional hazard of cars engaged in a practice for another rally. In spite of these problems the largest capacity cars had to maintain an average speed of no less than 60km/h (37mph). About a quarter of the 85 starters had retired by the end of the first day, and only 33 remained unpenalised. By the end of the third stage (Cortina to Menaggio), which included eight major passes and a special timed section to the summit of Stelvio, only 32 cars remained in contention – 17 of them British. Indeed, as the fifth stage (Aix-les-Bains to Cannes, including a timed test on the Col de l'Izoard) neared its end, it was evident that this was going to be a vintage year for Britain. The greatest triumph went to Ian Appleyard and his wife Pat, driving a Jaguar XK120 which was reputed to know its way along almost every road

ABOVE Ian Appleyard was one of only two drivers (the other was Stirling Moss) to win a Coupe des Alpes en Or for achieving three consecutive penalty-free Alpine runs (1950–2) in the post-war period. Here he takes his faithful Jaguar XK120 up the Giovo Pass (near Vipiteno) during the 1950 event.

LEFT With the growth in tourist traffic and the closing of all Swiss roads to motor sport during the 1960s, the Coupe des Alpes slowly contracted until, by 1971, it was confined to France. Rough roads became harder to find, and the easier terrain led to increasing dominance of the rally by fragile but fast sports cars. Bernard Darniche piloted this Alpine-Renault to victory in 1971. The Alpine, built around a highly tuned 140bhp version of Renault's 1.6-litre engine, proved a formidable rally contender.

in the Alps. The Appleyards had completed the rally with no demerits for the third year running, and so qualified for the most coveted of all the prizes – a Coupe des Alpes en Or. Three 2.3-litre Sunbeam-Talbot 90s took the team award, with drivers Stirling Moss, Mike Hawthorn, and George Murray Frame all with clean sheets; each also was therefore awarded a Coupe des Alpes (as the old Coupe des Glaciers was now called). Moss, incidentally, went on to become the only other winner of a Coupe des Alpes en Or, completing his hat-trick of wins in 1954. (It should be mentioned that Walter Delmar would have joined this celebrated duo if the gold cup had been awarded before World War II: he won a Coupe des Glaciers an unmatched *four* years on the trot, 1931–4.) Although ostensibly the Alpine Rally never had an outright winner, first place among the Coupe des Alpes awards was determined by a 'figure of merit', which was decided by results of the special tests. In 1952 the highest figure of merit went to the hill-climb specialist Alex von Falkenhausen in his BMW 328.

The Coupe des Alpes was eventually stifled by the enormous post-war boom in tourism. Even the highest passes became accessible to normal traffic, and it became too dangerous to hold a rally at a time of year when the route was crowded with coaches and private cars. During the 1960s the event was confined to minor Alpine roads in France; but even in this truncated form the hazards proved too great, and after one last try in 1971 the Alpine was finished. A great event, it has no equivalent in the present rally calendar.

As late as 1971 there were still a few lonely mountain roads in the Alpes Maritimes where Coupe des Alpes contenders could let themselves go without fear of bumping into tourist traffic. Here are two of the cars on different sections of the Col du Noyer. BELOW Christine Trautmann (Alpine-Renault). RIGHT Jean-François Piot and Jim Porter (Ford Escort), who took third place.

The RAC Rally

European rallying had become big business by the end of the 1950s: it attracted a large and knowledgeable following of spectators and considerable investment by the manufacturers in the development of cars and the provision of support teams. If it was to survive, however, a new format had to be devised; above all, events would have to be held either on carefully policed public roads or on private land. As it has turned out, the major European rallies have become a mixture of both these elements. This type of event evolved in Scandinavia. Drivers there found it was more fun to leave the public roads and drive through the vast evergreen forests where there was no other traffic, road surfaces were loose and interesting, and there were so many miles of track that it was almost impossible to get to know all the variations in any route. Gradually, events like the Thousand Lakes Rally of Finland and the Midnight Sun Rally of Sweden crystallised into a string of hectic special stages linked by more leisurely runs on public roads, where the low average speeds required could be achieved without putting normal traffic at risk. It was a formula which, given the availability of enough forest or other private roads, enabled really fast, competitive rallies to be organised. That was how the RAC Rally of Great Britain turned itself in 1960 from a middle-weight navigational exercise, with a few driving tests and some pleasant social overtones, into one of the toughest and most closely fought events in the calendar.

The RAC today consists of a series of special stages (mainly on Forestry Commission land in Yorkshire, Scotland, Wales, and elsewhere) linked by road sections. The rally is invariably won and lost on the special stages. A target time is set for each of these stages, but the time allowance is so miserly that each stage is effectively an individual race; the winner of the rally is the car which has accumulated the lowest aggregate of lateness penalties. Up to this point, then, the rally resembles the special stages of the Monte. It differs crucially from the Monte, however, in that the drivers are unfamiliar with the route: although the teams may know beforehand which forest tracks are going to be used for the special stages, they are not allowed to practise on them. They therefore cannot compile the 'pace notes' (descriptions of every detail of the route) which a co-driver on the Monte reads to his driver on the special stages. The RAC puts a premium on 20-20 vision, lightning reflexes, and brilliant car control.

The RAC is held in November, which means that the rough gravel or dirt surfaces of the forest tracks are likely to have a generous coating of ice or even snow in hilly regions. This, of course, is very much to the taste of the Scandinavians, and it is hardly surprising that, since the rally assumed its present form, Swedish and Finnish drivers have taken a firm grip on the trophy and have rarely let it go. The first, and one of the greatest, of these drivers was Erik Carlsson, a genial giant of a man who drove what might have seemed a rather uncompetitive car, the Saab 96. This was powered by a three-cylinder, two-stroke engine of only 850cc, but it had the cardinal rallying virtues of strength and stamina. Carlsson won the RAC in 1960 and 1961. By the time of the 1962 event the European championship had already been clinched by Eugen Böhringer (Mercedes-Benz), but the rallying world was agog to see if Böhringer could

RIGHT Map of the RAC Rally route in 1962.

BELOW Erik Carlsson was the greatest rally driver of the early 1960s and his string of international successes established the formidable reputation of the little 850cc Saab 96. Car and driver are seen here in the Monte Carlo Rally of 1962, which Carlsson won before going on to complete his hat-trick of RAC victories later in the year.

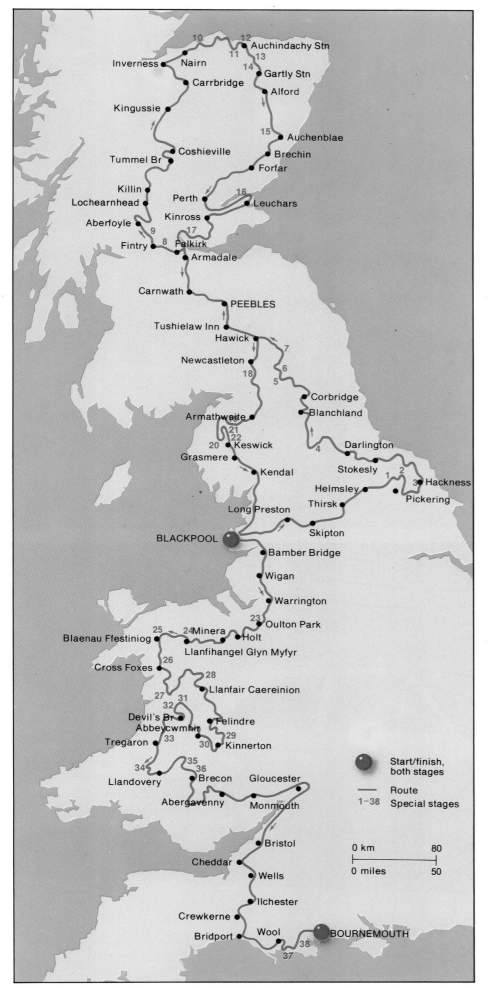

Inverness Nairn
10 12 Auchindachy Stn
11 13
14 Gartly Stn
Carrbridge
Alford
Kingussie
15 Auchenblae
Coshieville Brechin
Tummel Br Forfar
Killin
Lochearnhead Perth 16 Leuchars
Aberfoyle Kinross
9 17
Fintry 8 Falkirk
Armadale
Carnwath
PEEBLES
Tushielaw Inn
Hawick 7
Newcastleton
18 6
5
Corbridge
Blanchland
Armathwaite
21
22
20 Keswick 4 Darlington
Grasmere
Kendal Stokesly
1 2
Helmsley 3 Hackness
Thirsk Pickering
Long Preston
Skipton
BLACKPOOL
Bamber Bridge
Wigan
Warrington
23 Oulton Park
25 24 Minera
Blaenau Ffestiniog Holt
Llanfihangel Glyn Myfyr
Cross Foxes 26
28
Llanfair Caereinion
27 31
32
Devil's Br Felindre
Abbeycwmhir
Tregaron 33 29
30 Kinnerton
34 35
36
Llandovery Brecon Gloucester
Abergavenny Monmouth

Bristol
Cheddar
Wells
Ilchester
Crewkerne
Bridport Wool BOURNEMOUTH
38
37

Start/finish, both stages

Route
1–38 Special stages

0 km   80
0 miles   50

gild his crown with the RAC or Carlsson could achieve the hat-trick.

The rally had not at that time quite assumed its present form. There were still complicated navigational sections on minor roads, where it was not easy to keep to the 48.3km/h (30mph) average required. Carlsson was once again running with an expert British navigator (David Stone) because Scandinavian co-drivers would not have had the local knowledge to cope with this aspect of the event. There was also a clause in the rules forbidding organised assistance for drivers in terms of spare parts, repairs, and so on, but it was very much an open question as to what was meant by 'organised'. When the rally arrived at Helmsley in north Yorkshire, having crossed the Pennines from the starting point at Blackpool, it was seen that, by some wonderful accident, most of the manufacturers with cars in the rally had service vans and crews of mechanics standing by.

Soon afterwards, the real test, the forest driving, started in earnest. The first three special stages were at night in the dales around the old Yorkshire town of Pickering. The scene and atmosphere of such special stages are quite unlike those of the Monte or the Alpine: there is no snow, no vertiginous mountain passes. The forests are silent, the rough track not much wider than a large car and hemmed in by the tall, straight trees. Spectators are sprinkled thinly along the route, but congregate at the sharpest or trickiest corners – where their presence warns the drivers that they will need to take extra-special care. The tall trees deaden all noise, so that the cars appear without warning. To the uninitiated, they seem to be travelling at suicidal speed. Carlsson arrives, the little red Saab looking almost too small for its 20-stone driver, its two-stroke engine screaming like a bandsaw, and so highly tuned that it develops hardly any power below 5,000rpm. He is going much too fast to slow down for the corner: then the crowd realises that he does not need to – the car goes half sideways, the engine note hardly changes, and Carlsson takes the smoothest line through the curve and vanishes once more among the trees. It seems inconceivable that he has never driven down this road before; but that is the mark of the truly great forest-rally driver.

Others were less lucky. The forests were not Böhringer's favourite scene, and his Mercedes-Benz hit a tree in Staindale (the third special stage) and was out of the rally; the Morley brothers, Donald and his co-driver Erle – among the most successful British rally drivers of the time – rolled their Austin-Healey 3000 and retired; Peter Harper's Sunbeam Rapier hit an unseen rock after a fuse blew and extinguished his lights.

The rally wound north into Scotland through Peebles and Falkirk. By now it was obvious that impossible times were being set for some stages. Near Fintry, west of Falkirk, for instance, a dark, twisting, muddy track through a wood enclosing a reservoir had a target time of 7 minutes 15 seconds. Even Carlsson, who was going faster than anyone else, took more than two minutes longer on this, the eighth special stage. The route continued northward through Lochearnhead and Aviemore to Inverness. Carlsson's lead was impressive by now; behind him were two other

Swedes, Tom Trana and Bengt Söderström, both in Mini-Coopers, followed by Paddy Hopkirk and Pat Moss, both in Austin-Healey 3000s (unlikely seeming contenders on forest tracks, but very strong as well as fast).

From Inverness the route lay east and then south. On the 14th stage in Clashindarroch Forest (north of Alford) Carlsson almost came to grief when his Saab broke a suspension radius arm. There followed one of the classic little episodes in rallying history: big Erik had the good fortune to find a Saab 96 belonging to a spectator, who readily agreed to remove the needed component from his own car. The radius arm was quickly fitted at the roadside and Carlsson pressed on. On the next special stage, in Drumtochty Forest (north-east of Brechin), Carlsson's team-mate Olle Dahl had to retire when his works Saab 96 attacked a tree.

By the time the rally returned to Peebles four Scandinavian drivers were in the first five places; Paddy Hopkirk, the leading Briton, was running fourth. Pat Moss, in seventh place, was being strongly challenged for the ladies' prize by Sylvia Osterberg, the Swedish driver, in a 1.6-litre Volvo PV544 saloon. Already 35 cars had retired, and there were still more than 1,600km (1,000 miles) to go. It had rained unceasingly throughout the tour of Scotland, and it continued to rain as the cars picked their way along tracks-turned-quagmires in the Lake District forests. After an overnight stop

in Blackpool the cars proceeded to the circuit at Oulton Park, Cheshire, for a time trial. Only four drivers, including Pat Moss and Hopkirk, emerged without penalty. Carlsson dropped a single point, but was still in the lead.

From Oulton Park the drivers set off for the forests of north Wales. Here the conditions were so bad that one special stage was cancelled. But that still left the horrors of the special stages of Gwydir (near Llanrwst) and Coed-y-Brenin forest (north of Dolgellau), both of which accounted for more retirements; elsewhere, heavy frosts turned normal country roads into skating rinks. Through all these problems and awful driving conditions, Carlsson pressed calmly on. Of the drivers of the more powerful cars, only Pat Moss (who was to marry Carlsson the following year) made up much ground on the big Swede on the final run through Brecon, Gloucester, Cheddar, and Bridport to the finish at Bournemouth. She finished in third place. Paddy Hopkirk came second. But no one could catch Carlsson. He was the clear winner, and had made history with his third RAC in succession.

Carlsson's victory came at a time when rallying was fast changing its form. As the 'no-organised-assistance' rule of the 1962 event showed, there was still a feeling that a rally should be restricted to cars, drivers, and co-drivers contending with the conditions without any outside help. That feeling did not survive for long. The growing interest of the factory teams, who wanted to see

ABOVE The RAC draws large crowds of enthusiastic spectators who are prepared to stand all night in the middle of nowhere watching the cars dash by. Here some of them are silhouetted in a blaze of headlights on one of the special stages at Dalby (north of York) in the 1979 rally.

LEFT The Ford Escort RS1800, with a twin-cam engine developing up to 270bhp, was the most successful British rally car of the 1970s and had a string of victories in the RAC. Here Hannu Mikkola is on his way to winning the 1978 event.

their cars finish high in the order if not actually win, meant that official service points had to be recognised. Why, ran the argument, should a car be put out of the running by a single moment of bad luck when it had cost so much to prepare?

It is an argument which has gained force as the cars have become increasingly specialized and expensive. The modern rally car superficially resembles its showroom equivalent, apart from its special seats and extra instruments and lights. But in fact each works car is stripped down to its bare body shell and carefully reinforced in areas which might otherwise be weak, such as suspension mounting points. As it is rebuilt, fuel and brake lines are run through the body instead of underneath it to protect them from damage on rough tracks; it may also be fitted with an undershield to protect the engine sump. Meanwhile, the engine and gearbox are very carefully assembled, with moving parts fitted to much finer tolerances than on the standard road cars. Rally engines today are very highly modified and tuned, to the point where they give almost as much power as pure racing units. Gear ratios are selected to give maximum acceleration rather than an exceptionally high top speed, which is set by the red line on

the rev. counter. The gearing is varied to suit each type of rally. For the RAC type of event, the cars rarely need to better 160km/h (100mph). Weight saving is very important: reducing a typical car's weight by 25kg (56lb) is equivalent to adding about 10bhp to engine output. Useless interior trim is therefore stripped away, which has the effect of making the inside of the car very noisy. As a result, a standard fitting now is an aircraft-type intercom set with microphones and earphones for the driver and co-driver. Many cars also have VHF radio to enable a crew to keep in touch with its team manager and the service points.

Top-class rallying has become so specialised that cars will be prepared as 'forest' cars for events like the RAC Rally or 'tarmac' cars for the Monte Carlo Rally and similar events which are, in the main, run on hard-surfaced public roads. Much depends on the right choice of tyres: as long as a car is going well the main job of its service crews is to change its tyres to those most suitable for the next section. On the Monte Carlo Rally each team of cars will have dozens, even hundreds, of tyres distributed at points along the route; some will have studs fitted, others will offer a choice of tread compounds and patterns.

The Safari Rally

For the manager of a factory rally team, the ideal event is a European rally run over a fairly small area where there are plenty of public roads along which his service crews can take short cuts, so that they can always be in position before their cars arrive at the specified service points. His nightmare is a rally in another continent, with a route strung out along hundreds of miles of wilderness, and where communications are difficult or impossible if the weather turns foul. Such an event is the Safari Rally of Kenya. Nightmare it may be, but it has gained such status and international popularity that the main factory teams cannot afford to miss it.

The Safari started life in 1953 as a competitive run to celebrate the Coronation of Queen Elizabeth II. It caught the public imagination as an event which in some ways harked back to the brave pioneering days of rallying: thousands of miles of unmade, dusty roads almost empty of traffic, along which impossible schedules could be demanded of the competing cars. It was not quite a race, but the fastest surviving car was certainly the winner. Survival, however, was obviously the name of the game. There was the weather, which could change from sweltering, dusty heat to tropical monsoon with bewildering speed. There were the animals: out in the bush the elephants, giraffes, and lions presented more of a hazard than any local traffic (in 1963 Erik Carlsson was leading the rally when his Saab was put out of commission after hitting an aardvark). The native Africans have also varied in their response to the sight of cars careering at breakneck speed across the bush, frightening children and livestock.

Centred on the Kenyan capital, Nairobi, the rally originally ran also through parts of neighbouring Uganda and Tanzania. More recently, political tensions have resulted in first Tanzania

RIGHT For long the Safari Rally was dominated by local drivers in durable saloon cars. The winner of the 1968 event – one of the toughest in the rally's history – was the Peugeot 404 of Nick Nowicki and Paddy Cliff. The 404 established a remarkable record in the Safari, its sheer strength and ability to keep going through deep mud bringing it several wins.

BELOW Second-placed car in the 1968 event was the Lotus-Cortina driven by Peter Huth and Ian Grant, another pair of local drivers. Although much faster than the Peugeot, their car was plagued by mechanical disasters, including a damaged front suspension.

and later Uganda withdrawing their hospitality, and the rally is now confined to Kenya. This still gives it an awful lot of room for manoeuvre, although there are signs that some of its favourite sections are becoming better known to the professional rally teams. The cars, too, are now better prepared, tougher and with greater ground clearance, while the ultra-quick European crews have learned enough about the conditions to be able to win without local assistance.

In earlier times, this was far from the case. Indeed, there was at one time a firm conviction that the Safari could be won only by a local crew, or at least by a crew with at least one local man who knew the roads and how to cope with the violent changes in weather. Certainly, familiarity with conditions gives the locals a useful edge over visiting Europeans: they know how to negotiate a deep ford in a fast-flowing river, for example, or whether it is worth making a detour through the bush to avoid a particularly thick patch of mud. In the early days the locals also knew which cars stood the best chance of winning, because they drove them all the year round. Thus the first decade of the Safari was the years of the Volkswagen, the big, simple British Fords, and above all, perhaps, the Peugeot 404.

There were years, however, when the conditions were too much even for the most skilful and rugged local heroes. Such a year was 1963, when only seven out of the original 84 starters were classified as finishers. The winners that year were Nick Nowicki and Paddy Cliff, a pair of Kenya-based drivers in a Peugeot 404. They fought their way through torrential rain, washed-away roads, thick mud, and quicksand to take a prize which even then was extremely coveted.

Five years later, they were again among the entrants in another Safari that was destined to have only seven finishers. There were 91 entrants for the 1968 rally, including works teams from BMC and Ford. The Abingdon-based BMC rally headquarters had sent Timo Mäkinen in what was reputed to be an extremely tough Austin/Morris 1800 (nicknamed the Land Crab in rallying circles). Ford relied for the most part on the skilful local drivers Vic Preston and Robin Ullyate, but

also sent out the European ace Bengt Söderström. Peugeot 404s were there in strength, and so were the boxy Datsun 510 saloons which were beginning to make an impression on the East African motoring scene.

The rally consisted of two legs, both of them starting and finishing at Nairobi. The first leg ran north and west of Nairobi over the Mau Narok escarpment, and west through Kakamega to the Uganda frontier at Busia. After passing through Jinja and Kampala it returned by a long northerly loop taking in Toroio, Kitale, Nakuru, and the lower slopes of Mount Kenya. The leg, which included 40 control points, was 2,300km (1,428 miles) long. The southern leg, south and east of Nairobi, passed through Kajiado, Makindu, Bura, and Mariakani to Mombasa; then it struck south into Tanzania, past Tanga and on to Korogwe. From here the route made a huge loop to the south, taking in Dar-es-Salaam and Mvomero before returning to Korogwe, then struck north-west to Nairobi via Kisiwani, Moshi, Arusha, Namanga, and Kajiado. This leg had 35 control points and measured 2,650km (1,646 miles). The extreme difficulty of the route was made yet more formidable by the series of quite unrealistic time allowances between each control point and by the fact that about two thirds of the total mileage had to be driven at night.

Even before the start the weather took a hand: the monsoon had arrived early and there were reports of floods from many parts of the route. As the cars left Nairobi behind, the drivers soon found conditions to be even worse than they had feared. There was water and mud everywhere, often deep enough to conceal huge rocks and tree stumps. Suspensions and transmissions took a fearful hammering. Mäkinen dropped out early,

Map of the 1968 rally. At that time the Safari route spread beyond the frontiers of Kenya into Uganda and Tanganyika. Today it is confined to Kenya, but it has lost none of its car-destroying toughness.

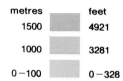

metres	feet
1500	4921
1000	3281
0–100	0–328

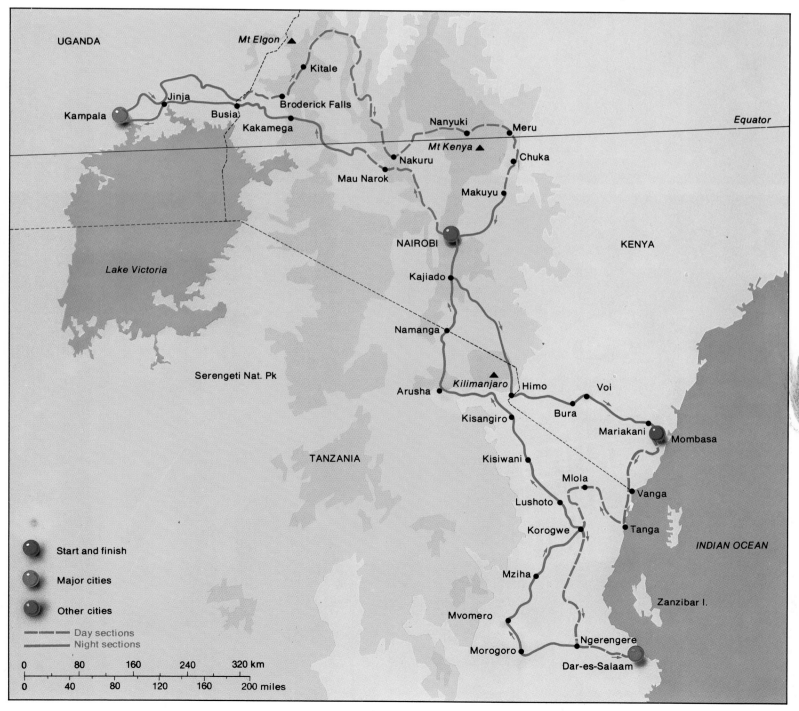

UGANDA
Mt Elgon ▲
Kitale
Jinja
Kampala
Busia
Broderick Falls
Kakamega
Nanyuki
Meru
Equator
Mt Kenya ▲
Chuka
Nakuru
Mau Narok
Makuyu
NAIROBI
KENYA
Kajiado
Lake Victoria
Namanga
Serengeti Nat. Pk
Kilimanjaro ▲
Himo
Voi
Arusha
Kisangiro
Bura
Mariakani
Mombasa
TANZANIA
Kisiwani
Mlola
Vanga
Lushoto
Korogwe
Tanga
INDIAN OCEAN
Mziha
Zanzibar I.
Mvomero
Ngerengere
Morogoro
Dar-es-Salaam

● Start and finish
● Major cities
● Other cities
--- Day sections
─── Night sections

| 0 | 80 | 160 | 240 | 320 km |
| 0 | 40 | 80 | 120 | 160 | 200 miles |

his 1800 snapping its drive shafts when struggling up Mau Narok. By the time the rally reached the Uganda capital of Kampala 26 cars had retired. Not only the weather was to blame: on the return loop to Busia, Pat Moss ran her Renault 16 into a wall of rocks some disenchanted Ugandans had built across the road. By the end of the northern leg only 22 cars were in any state to continue. The leader was the Datsun of local driver Joginder Singh (a previous winner) and V. Smith.

With so few survivors, and with conditions on the southern loop reported to be even worse than those on the northern, the Safari organisers had to take steps to ensure they had a finisher to claim their trophy. The maximum lateness at controls was extended from four hours to eight, and some

of the worst roads in Tanzania were cut from the route. For many competitors, it was still not enough. Where the route ran close to the Indian Ocean, from Mombasa down towards Tanzania, Söderström's Cortina became completely trapped in deep mud and could not be pulled clear. The Peugeot 404 of Bert Shankland (who had already won the rally twice before) hit a tree stump submerged in the mud and practically wrecked its front suspension. Shankland knocked the wheels more or less straight with a sledge-hammer and pressed on, only to have the front end of the car break away completely when he was only about 320km (200 miles) from the finish.

The destruction continued. There had been 21 cars out of Nairobi, but only 17 reached Mombasa.

BELOW From the early 1960s Japanese car manufacturers boosted sales in East African markets by entering works teams in the Safari. The way was pioneered by Datsun. It was followed in 1977 with victory by this little Colt Lancer driven by the Sikh Joghinder Singh, a local driver with a remarkable record of success in the rally.

LEFT Safari 1975: co-driver Chris Bates sprints to a control point to have his route card stamped; Tanzanian driver Bert Shankland waits behind the wheel of the Peugeot 504, which came fifth.

BELOW The European breakthrough in the Safari came in 1972, when this Ford Escort of Hannu Mikkola and Gunner Palm won.

As they went south through Korogwe in Tanzania there were 13; when they returned through Korogwe on the return run from the deeper south, there were only eight. All the survivors were local drivers, notable among them being the all-woman crew of Lucille Cardwell and Mrs Gerry Davies in their Datsun.

Through most of the Tanzanian section the lead was held by Peter Huth in his powerful Lotus-Cortina, but the car was not running well; an emergency windscreen had to be roped on after the car had rolled over, and its front suspension began to look as dilapidated as that of Shankland's Peugeot. Huth fought back to take the lead for a time, and was in fact the first car to return to Nairobi. He had not won, however. Throughout the last few hundred kilometres in Kenya, Nowicki and Cliff mounted a relentless and carefully calculated attack on their rivals, their Peugeot 404 running much more sweetly than any other car left in the rally. They arrived second in Nairobi, but were comfortably ahead of Huth on points. Behind Huth were five other heroic crews: Kim Mandeville's Triumph 2000 was third; Mike Armstrong's Peugeot 404 was fourth; Joginder Singh's Datsun was fifth; Robin Ullyate was sixth in a Cortina GT; and Lucille Cardwell survived in her Datsun, thanks to the organisers' decision to extend the maximum lateness allowance to no less than 12 hours.

There have been several great Safari rallies since then, though none that was quite as much of a struggle. Following Hannu Mikkola's win in 1972 – the first by a non-local driver – the European factory teams have been readier to send out their top drivers and to back them with thorough service, often controlled from light aeroplanes and using two-way radio to talk to the team cars, as Ford's team manager Stuart Turner first did when he master-minded the Mikkola win.

The cost of mounting a team effort on this scale thousands of miles from 'home base' is immense. But for the successful manufacturers the rewards of success in terms of car sales – not only in Africa but throughout the 'Third World' – are immense. Unlike sports-car and *grand-prix* racers, rally cars at least *look* something like the models one can buy in the High Street showroom, and the sales 'spin-off' from the successful rally cars is now too great to be ignored by the major firms.

The Safari nowadays attracts exotic sporting machinery as well as the more durable saloons.

INSET Like some other low-slung sports cars, Sandro Munari's Lancia Stratos, seen here in 1977 when it came third behind a Ford Escort and a Datsun Violet, was provided with increased ground-clearance and chassis reinforcement to cope with the terrain.

MAIN PICTURE Mercedes-Benz made a comeback to world-championship rallying in 1979, and three of their cars finished in the first six in the Safari. Here is one of the 280E saloons, piloted by Joghinder Singh, a new recruit to Mercedes' works team.

Sports Car Classics

Historically, a sports car has been easier to recognise than to define. Until World War I, cars used for sporting events were either out-and-out racers or 'tourers' – fast, open cars, usually with four seats rather than two. We usually think of a sports car as a two-seater; but in the early 1920s, when the term 'sports car' was first used widely, even *grand-prix* cars invariably had two seats and were usually 'street legal' (permitted to be driven on public roads).

In general, the differences between sports cars and *grand-prix* cars have had more to do with mechanical specification than with appearance. But there has long been a distinction between the types of race in which each took part. *Grands prix* have evolved into relatively brief events on a short circuit. The classic sports-car events have been run over far longer distances or on longer and more difficult circuits, and they have generally provided a more searching test of strength and endurance for both driver and car. There have been many famous sports-car races, but three have stood head and shoulders above the rest: the Targa Florio; the Mille Miglia, and the Le Mans 24-hours. . . .

Targa Florio

The Targa Florio was the first of the three sports-car classics. It was inaugurated in 1906 and was the inspiration of one man, Vincenzo Florio, a wealthy Sicilian merchant. For many years it was open to every type of car – *grand-prix* racers as well as tourers and, later, sports cars. It took place on public roads in the Madonie mountains of north-central Sicily, which in the early years of this century was a wild region where civilization had touched more lightly than in most of Europe. The roads on the island, and especially in the mountains, were appalling – little more than narrow, serpentine tracks in the countryside, and little wider or better-surfaced when negotiating the villages on the route. Three circuits were used at various times: the Piccolo Madonie of 72km (44.6 miles), the Medio Madonie of 108km (67 miles), and the Grande Madonie of 148.8km (92.3 miles); the number of laps varied, in different years, from three to eight.

Originally, the start/finish line and grandstands were at Buonfornello on the island's main north-coast road. From there the Piccolo Madonie ran south to Cerda, then through Caltavuturo and Collesano in the mountains, and northwards to the north-coast village of Campofelice, from which there was a final dash westward to Buonfornello. The Medio and Grande circuits involved sinuous extensions to the Piccolo Madonie in the mountains between Caltavuturo and Collesano.

The formidable difficulties of the Targa are evident in the average speeds of the winners, which were astonishingly low compared with those of other major sports-car races of the time. Felice Nazzaro, the winner in 1907, averaged just over 50km/h (31mph); but it was not until 1924 that the winner bettered 65km/h (40mph), and it was only in 1953 that the average exceeded 80km/h (50mph). The many corners – the Medio Madonie was reputed to have more than 1,500! – the gradients, and, not least, the unprotected nature of much of the circuit all conspired to hold down speeds; yet one of the more cunning features of all three circuits was the great open stretch of

PRECEDING TWO PAGES Le Mans pit area during the night stages of the famous 24-hour race.

BELOW The rough mountain roads of Sicily tested cars and drivers to the full in the early years of the Targa Florio. Here Vincenzo Trucco powers his Isotta-Fraschini around a hairpin on his way to victory in 1908.

straight road from Campofelice to Buonfornello, for which the cars had to be properly geared if they were not to lose time or risk blowing up their engines beyond the design speed.

One of the greatest drives ever seen in the Targa Florio was in 1919, when the Medio Madonie was used for the first time. The entry was small but of high quality. The hot favourite was the Frenchman, René Thomas (later to become a great hill-climb specialist), in a 4.9-litre, eight-cylinder Ballot. Two 4.5-litre Fiat *grand-prix* cars were entered by wealthy Italian enthusiasts, and there were also two 8.5-litre *grand-prix* Italas. Beside these giants the 4-cylinder, 2.5-litre Peugeot L25s looked almost insignificant; they were in any case five years old, having been built in 1914 but never raced before because of the war. One of the Peugeot drivers was André Boillot, the younger brother of Georges Boillot, the greatest French racing driver of the pre-war era.

The race took place in November, often a stormy season in Sicily. The weather was mild at Buonfornello, but to the south snow lay on the mountains, which were wreathed in storm clouds. The cars were flagged away at short intervals – the first to go being young Enzo Ferrari (in a CMN), who was later to build the great sports cars that bear his name. It was almost two hours before the first cars to depart returned to Buonfornello. René Thomas had to pull into the pits after completing his first lap, his water tank having boiled dry after

the fan belt had broken. Thomas reported that road conditions in the mountains were truly dreadful, with 5km (3 miles) of the highest part of the circuit deep in snow. On the lower stretches the problem was mud and stones, which was evident in the appearance of the crews, who looked like mud statues as they roared past.

Thomas appeared to have done exceptionally well, driving the first lap over 10 minutes faster than any of the other cars to come through before him. Then André Boillot appeared and it was seen that he had driven the first lap four minutes faster than Thomas, and almost a quarter of an hour quicker than the next competitor. Even as the crowd watched and cheered, Boillot showed just how hard he was trying. He skidded to the outside of the road just past the pits and ended up with the Peugeot stuck, having almost gone over the edge into a ditch. He and his riding mechanic had to get out and manhandle the car back onto the road. Five times more Boillot was to have such close encounters with disaster, for he was driving like a man possessed.

Thomas stopped for fuel at the end of the second lap, to learn at last how hard he was being challenged. Boillot did not stop: instead a 35-litre (7.7gal) can of petrol was thrown into the Peugeot as it went past the pits, and his riding mechanic emptied it into the tank on the move. Boillot was now seven minutes ahead of Thomas, but every second was vital: at last the weather was improv-

The narrow, winding streets of small towns and villages lent character (and often threatened disaster) to the Targa. Nando Minoia's Isotta hurtles past stone walls, balcony spectators, and a *carabiniere* in Collesano during the 1907 race. Minoia took second place to Felice Nazzaro's FIAT.

ing, and as the roads dried out it was expected that Thomas's bigger car would have the advantage. Things did not seem to be working out that way: after three laps, the Peugeot's lead was up to 11 minutes. There was one lap to go, and Thomas now stepped up his challenge, determined to wipe out Boillot's lead as road conditions improved. But he tried too hard: the Ballot skidded, hit a marker stone, and broke its differential.

At last the spectators at the finish saw Boillot heading for the line. They pressed forward too eagerly, blocking the road. Boillot jammed on his brakes, spun wildly, and hit one of the temporary grandstands, coming to rest in a pile of wood and canvas. By some miracle, nobody was hurt, but Boillot was still 10m from the finishing line. He and his mechanic were extracted from the wreckage and placed in their seats, the engine was started, and the Peugeot backed over the line, apparently to win. Alas, it was not as easy as that. Somebody pointed out that it was against the rules to finish in reverse gear, and so the crew had to drive back some 30m along the course, turn the car round, and cross the line forwards! 'C'est pour la France', André Boillot is reported to have muttered as he sat there on the verge of collapse, his victory gained at last.

It was a different story altogether in another epic year, 1930. French Bugatti Type 35s (which were built in both *grand-prix* and sports-car form and were the finest racers of the late 1920s) had won the Targa Florio for five years running, from 1925 to 1929, and this was more than Italian pride could bear. In 1930 there was yet another strong Bugatti team entry, including Louis Chiron and Albert Divo, two of the greatest French drivers of the day, the latter of whom had won the two previous Targas. Against this formidable team were pitted the Alfa Romeos, whose drivers (we can see with the benefit of hindsight) were more formidable still: the legendary triumvirate of Achille Varzi, Giuseppe Campari, and Tazio Nuvolari.

This was a typical Targa Florio, unlike that of November 1919: it was May and the sun was shining. It warmed the crowds who lined the narrow village streets, but it made the going uncomfortably hot for the crews in the open cockpits of their powerful cars. Alfa Romeo had intended to enter two of the supercharged 2-litre, straight-eight P2 *grand-prix* cars, one for Varzi and the other for Campari; but the huge Giuseppe was so concerned about the heat that his car was changed to the lighter and more comfortable 6C-1750, one of a range of classic Alfa sports cars of that era. Varzi was determined to drive the P2, however: he had bought the racer from Campari in 1928, before he had joined the Alfa team; although now a veteran, it had served him well.

It was a desperate battle. Bugatti lost Divo's car when a valley echo convinced the driver he was being closely followed: he turned to look, his attention strayed for a second, and that was enough to send him crashing into the parapet of a bridge, tearing off a wheel. Louis Chiron, driving to orders to play it safe for the first part of the race, suddenly found himself carrying the Bugatti standard and with time to make up. He began to drive on the limit, but was hampered by his young and

ABOVE André Boillot in the 2.5-litre Peugeot he piloted to victory in the epic Targa of 1919.

RIGHT Even the fastest post-war sports-racing cars, such as this V12 Ferrari 275P2 in the hands of Sicilian driver Nino Vaccarella, were hard put to better an average speed of 100km/h (62mph).

BELOW In spite of the challenging nature of its circuits, the Targa claimed only one fatality in its long history, when in 1925 Count Giulio Masetti overturned this 1.5-litre, eight-cylinder Delage Grand Prix.

inexperienced riding mechanic, who began to feel ill. Thus distracted, Chiron skidded and hit a retaining wall guarding the edge of the road, damaging two wheels which had to be changed before he could continue.

Behind him, it was clear that only Varzi's Alfa P2 had enough power and speed to beat Chiron, despite his stop. But Varzi's car was in trouble: his spare wheel had fallen off, tearing a small hole in the fuel tank on the way. Low on fuel, Varzi stopped to grab a can from one of the Alfa Romeo replenishment stations, intending that his mechanic should pour it in on the move, as Boillot's had done 11 years before. The fuel spilled over the Alfa's tail and caught alight on the exhaust. Flames licked around the car, but, with victory in sight, Varzi refused to stop, crouching forward to give his mechanic more room to beat out the fire with his seat cushion. At last they came to the final long straight from Campofelice to Buonfornello, and Varzi, ignoring the engine's speed limit, kept his foot hard down for the 8km (5-mile) sprint to the finish. He beat Chiron by less than two minutes, but he had set a trend: Alfa Romeos were to win the next five Targa Florios, Varzi himself winning again in 1934 and Nuvolari in 1931 and 1932.

In the great years between the two wars, it was Bugatti against Alfa Romeo; and after 1955 (when Stirling Moss and Peter Collins prevailed in a Mercedes-Benz 300SLR) until the final race in 1973, the Targa Florio was virtually monopolised by Porsche and Ferrari, the German marque proving the more dominant. The Targa was killed by the enormous growth of tourism in Sicily. Even the remoter parts of the circuits were accessible to holidaymakers' cars, and the government was disinclined to close them to traffic for the duration of the race.

Even in its final years the Targa retained its unique atmosphere, especially in the villages on the circuit, where spectators were often almost close enough to touch the cars as they roared by.

ABOVE The Giovanni Boeris/Piero Monticone 1.6-litre Chevron B21 closes on the Günther Steckkönig/Giulio Pucci Porsche 911 Carrera RSR at a hairpin in Collesano in 1973.

LEFT Sandra Munari (best known as one of the greatest Italian rally drivers) takes the winning Ferrari 312P through the little square in Campofelice in 1972.

Mille Miglia

Mainland Italy's classic road race, the Mille Miglia (which means '1,000 miles'), was similar in concept to the Targa Florio, except that it took in much of the northern half of Italy, was run on many of the country's major trunk roads, and passed through several great cities, including Rome, Florence, Bologna, and Verona. Unlike that of the Targa, the Mille Miglia's route – although never closed to the public during the race – put a premium on sheer speed as well as endurance, and some truly astonishing race averages were recorded during its comparatively brief but glorious history from 1927 to 1957.

The event was sponsored originally by the Brescia Automobile Club, and it always started and finished in the Piazza Vittoria in the centre of this northern Italian city. The 24 races were virtually an Italian benefit: Alfa Romeo won it 11 times (1928–30, 1932–8, and 1947), Ferrari eight times (1948–53 and 1956–7), and Lancia once (1954). Many of the great Italian drivers of the period took part in it – Nuvolari and Varzi each won it twice and Campari once before the war; Luigi Villoresi, Alberto Ascari, Eugenio Castelotti, and Piero Taruffi each succeeded once in the post-war years. It was also won no fewer

than four times by Carlo Biondetti (1938 and 1947–9), who also won the Targa Florio in 1948–9 and was the outstanding sports-car driver of his generation.

Apart from the 1940 event, when the race was shortened to a fraction of its normal length, the Mille Miglia was won only twice by foreign cars – each time victory going to Mercedes-Benz. The first of these German victories was in 1931, when the great Rudolf Caracciola (a German despite his name) won in a Ferdinand Porsche-designed Mercedes SSKL, with a supercharged 7.1-litre, eight-cylinder engine developing no less than 300hp. He covered the opening 209km (129 miles) from Brescia to Bologna at an average speed of 154.2km/h (95.8mph) – but at the end of the race was only 11 minutes ahead of Campari's Alfa-Romeo 6C-1750, whose engine had only a quarter the capacity of the giant Mercedes.

In 1955, in spite of the post-war Italian domination of the race, Mercedes-Benz was again expected to win. The marque had already proved almost invincible in *grand-prix* and sports-car racing in 1954, and its Mille Miglia team consisted of the already legendary Juan Manuel Fangio, together with Stirling Moss, Karl Kling, and Hans Herrmann, all driving the very fast Mercedes-Benz 300SLR fuel-injected eight-cylinder sports-racing models. The route went clockwise around Italy, taking in Verona, Vicenza, Padua, Ferrara, Ravenna, Rimini, Ancona, Pescara, the mountainous region around Popoli, Rieti, and Terni, then Rome, Siena, Florence, over the Appennini mountains to Bologna, then north-westward through Modena, Parma, Piacenza, and Mantua, and finally back to Brescia.

The contestants were allowed to drive solo if they wished. Most of the Italian drivers, and also Fangio, opted to do so in order to save weight. Moss, on the other hand, produced what amounted to a secret weapon in the form of a small, bearded, bespectacled man called Denis Jenkinson, who was an experienced side-car passenger in motor-cycle racing. Jenkinson's role was purely as a navigator. He had studied the route in the smallest detail and had reduced it to a series of notes describing every corner, junction, crest, or other feature. The notes were transcribed onto a long roll of paper, so that Jenkinson could literally wind his way along the route, reading aloud all the way; and Moss could drive that much faster because Jenkinson would be telling him the radius and camber of each bend and what lay on the other side of each crest. (It was a system which later became refined into the rally co-driver's pace notes, but the 1955 Mille Miglia saw its first serious use.)

Spectators along the route could judge the relative placings of the cars as they roared past because the race number painted on each corresponded to the time it was flagged away from Brescia. Moss was the last to leave, his number (722) indicating that he started at 07.22. Before long the fastest cars were neatly spaced out along the route, the early leaders being Moss, Taruffi in a 3.8-litre Ferrari Tipo 118LM, Herrmann, and Castelotti in a 4.4-litre Ferrari Tipo 121LM. Taruffi, indeed, led for most of the way to Pescara, on the east coast, which he reached at the remarkable average speed of 188km/h (117mph). By Rome, however, Moss was fractionally in the lead. He had completed the first 805km (500 miles) of the race, including the tortuous Gran Sasso mountain section between Pescara and Rome, in almost exactly five hours! Clearly Jenkinson's pace notes were proving invaluable over the trickiest sections of the route.

There was a Mille Miglia legend that the leader at Rome never won the race – but either nobody had told Moss or he was not superstitious. He was right not to be, for the Ferrari threat suddenly faded on the long stretches north of Rome, where Taruffi's engine suddenly lost its oil pressure. (The Italian was to have consolation of a kind two years later, when he would win the last Mille Miglia of all.) Moss now began to pull away from the rest of the field. His Mercedes team-mates, however, were in trouble: Herrmann retired with a holed fuel tank and Kling suffered from mechanical failure. Fangio's car seems to have been out of sorts from the start, but the Argentinian maestro was unequalled in his ability to 'nurse' a sick racer, and he steadily pressed on, picking up place after place as those in front of him faltered or dropped out.

By mid-afternoon the streets of Brescia thronged with thousands of spectators and the Piazza Vittoria was jam-packed. Telephone messages came into race control from farther down the route, but most of the onlookers found it easier to keep track of the race by listening to the radios in the cafés and bars. It seemed as though the Mille Miglia was the only programme that was being broadcast, and the messages all sounded much the same: 'Moss is in Cremona.' 'Moss is in Mantua.' 'Moss is in Montechiari.' The hoped-for Italian victory was not going to happen, but nobody seemed to mind.

Shortly after 17.30 the silver Mercedes-Benz 300SLR flashed through the city streets, into the crowded piazza, and across the finishing line. It was done with a flourish, although there was really no need. Moss had averaged 157km/h (97.9mph) and he was more than half an hour ahead of the second car, Fangio's similar Mercedes; Umberto Maglioli's Ferrari was the only other car to beat 11 hours for the distance. It was one of the greatest virtuoso performances in sports-car history, and Moss's average speed was to remain a record.

The Mille Miglia came to a tragic end in 1957, when the Marquis de Portago and Edward Nelson's Ferrari crashed into roadside spectators, killing both drivers and 11 other people.

Arguably Stirling Moss's greatest racing achievement was his victory in the Mille Miglia of 1955. With the help of detailed 'pace notes' from his navigator, spade-bearded Denis Jenkinson, Moss set a record average speed in his Mercedes-Benz 300SLR, a car modelled closely on the W196 *grand-prix* racer. Moss crowned this year with victories in the Targa Florio and the Tourist Trophy race.

Le Mans

The Le Mans 24-hour sports-car race is the great survivor. In spite of the fact that in recent years the rules of the race have altered so as to make it ineligible for the world sports-car championship, and in spite of the fact that it has been the scene of motor sport's most tragic disaster, its prestige remains so great that car manufacturers and drivers are obliged (some less than enthusiastically) to participate in it. In purely practical terms, its survival has hinged partly on the fact that, although it is run on public roads, the circuit is closed to normal traffic for the duration of the race.

Le Mans, which lies about 180km (112 miles) south-west of Paris, has long been a centre of French motor sport; as we shall see in Chapter 4, it was the scene of the first-ever *grand prix* in 1906. The circuit for the 24-hour race, immediately to the south of the city's southern suburb of Pontlieue, has been modified several times over the years but its general layout is as follows. From the start/finish line and pits at the north-west corner of the circuit the road curves eastwards into the Esses (a series of S-bends), and then turns sharp right at Le Tertre Rouge corner. From here the long Mulsanne straight runs south to Mulsanne corner, where it turns sharp right (westward) and continues through the fast Indianapolis bends to Arnage corner, the slowest on the circuit. From here the route lies northward, through a series of fast bends and corners, including that at Maison Blanche (White House), until it returns to the pits and grandstand area. The total length of the circuit is 13.3km (8.3 miles). The Mulsanne straight, and the sharp right-hand corner at its far end, are the dominant features of the circuit. The straight nowadays sees the fastest speeds attained in road racing (including *grands prix*) – many cars achieving more than 370km/h (230mph) – and this determines the gearing chosen; the approach to Mulsanne corner, which the cars have to negotiate at a relative crawl, puts enormous stresses on brakes and suspensions. The remorseless repetition of this cycle of immensely high speed followed by hard braking over the full 24-hour period is in large measure responsible for the high rate of retirement of cars during the race.

The inaugural race was in 1923. Its history has been distinguished by periods of several con-

ABOVE Le Mans 1925: the winner, Gérard de Courcelles' Lorraine-Diétrich, and the second-placed S.C.H. Davis/Jean Chassagne Sunbeam overtake a Chenard-Walcker (no. 49).

BELOW The winning 3-litre Bentley in the pits before the 1927 race.

secutive years when particular marques seem to have been unbeatable. Equally remarkable is the fact that the Bugatti Type 35, one of the greatest sports and racing cars of the 1920s and a consistent winner of the Targa Florio and other sports-car events and of many *grands prix*, never won the Le Mans. The first marque to dominate the event was Bentley, which won in 1924 and 1927–30.

Every car enthusiast knows that 1927 was the year of the multiple crash at the White House. The Bentley factory had spent two years in vainly trying to repeat its 1924 victory, and in 1927 it entered two of the faithful four-cylinder 3-litre cars and a new four-cylinder 4.5-litre model, which was expected to win if all went well. For the first five hours everything went according to the Bentley plan. Then, just as night closed in, and the three Bentleys, led by the 4.5-litre driven by L.G. Callingham, were out in front, a 2-litre Th. Schneider crashed at the White House corner, partly blocking the road. Callingham saw the obstruction too late, swerved to avoid it, and crashed on the other side of the road; George Duller, in the first 3-litre Bentley, was following too close and crashed into the 4.5-litre (Duller, a former steeplechase jockey, was catapulted over the roadside hedge). S.C.H. (Sammy) Davis in the third Bentley, 'Old No. 7', saw the danger quicker but could not avoid going broadside into the pile-up. The first two Bentleys were done for, but Davis

managed to nurse his car back to the pits, where it was hastily patched up. Meanwhile, a 3-litre Ariès driven by Robert Laly and Jean Chassagne took the lead. Through much of the night and the following day Davis and his co-driver 'Doc' Benjafield (the car's owner) pursued the Ariès. The French car retained a comfortable lead until more than 22 of the 24 hours had elapsed. Then quite suddenly it was put out of the race by a seized camshaft, and the Bentley hobbled home at an average speed of 98.7km/h (61.2mph), having completed 2,369.8km (1,469.3 miles).

The Bentley years were followed at Le Mans – as in the Targa Florio and the Mille Miglia – by a period of absolute dominance by the classic Alfa Romeo sports cars designed by Vittorio Jano. For the 1931 race, with the Bentley team having withdrawn from racing, Ettore Bugatti must have thought his chance had come. He fielded his superb Type 51s, similar to the 2.3-litre supercharged Type 35B but with double rather than single overhead camshafts. Their drivers included Louis Chiron and Albert Divo. In an otherwise moderate field, the chief dangers to the Bugattis seemed likely to be the massively powerful but not very agile Mercedes-Benz SSK driven by Henri Stoffel and Boris Ivanowski, and two supercharged Alfa Romeo 8C-2300s driven by Lord Howe and Sir Henry (Tim) Birkin and by Attilio Marinoni and Geofredo Zehender. Birkin was no

ABOVE LEFT 'Tim' Birkin (Alfa Romeo 8C-2300) leads Henri Stoffel (Mercedes-Benz SSK) out of Le Tertre Rouge corner and onto the Mulsanne Straight during the 1931 event. The 8C-2300 model (eight cylinders, 2.3 litres) in various hands won this and the three following Le Mans 24-hour races.

ABOVE RIGHT Birkin and his co-driver Lord Howe sip champagne after their epic victory.

stranger to Le Mans, having co-driven the winning Bentley in 1929; Marinoni had co-driven winning Alfas in the Spa 24-hour races of 1929 and 1930.

Chiron led from the start, followed by the Mercedes, then Divo in the second Bugatti, then the Howe/Birkin Alfa Romeo. The weather was extremely hot, and most of the drivers were worried about their tyres. The thought of tyre failure may have weighed heavily on Chiron's mind, for quite early in the race he got his braking wrong at Mulsanne corner at the end of the straight; the Mercedes shot into the lead and Chiron found he could not regain it. Soon, all was thrown into confusion as the expected tyre trouble began. First the Mercedes and then Chiron's Bugatti pulled into the pits with shredded tyres; Chiron had lost a good deal of time limping round to the pits after his tyre had failed on the Mulsanne straight on the opposite side of the circuit. The Howe/Birkin Alfa Romeo stopped for minor adjustments, letting Marinoni's Alfa through into the lead. Chiron got going again, then burst a second tyre. Soon afterwards came the news that a third Bugatti, driven by Maurice Rost, had suffered a tyre burst at Mulsanne and had rolled over the bank and into the forest, throwing its driver clear but killing an onlooker. All the Bugattis were withdrawn from the race.

The big Mercedes burst two more tyres, lost a great deal of ground by driving more slowly to try

to preserve the treads, and after a conference in the pits the team decided to change to Dunlop tyres. Marinoni's Alfa held the lead for much of the night but was eventually passed by the Howe/Birkin car. In attempting to regain his position Marinoni's much less experienced co-driver Zehender crashed at Arnage corner just as dawn was breaking. Alfa's hopes now rested on the British crew, who were anxiously aware of the renewed challenge of the Stoffel/Ivanowski Mercedes, which was going ominously well on its Dunlop tyres. The two cars made an interesting contrast. The big and heavy SSK relied mainly on brute power and speed: with 225bhp from its supercharged 7.1-litre engine, it had an advantage of no less than 70bhp over the Alfa and could expect to gain on its rival on the high-speed sections of the circuit, notably Mulsanne straight and the long run from Arnage corner to the pits. The Alfa, in the tradition of Jano's classic designs, relied on superlative road-holding and stamina.

Throughout the morning and early afternoon the SSK fought its way past the lesser contenders and regained second place. But it could not make good the time lost earlier through tyre trouble. As the race drew towards its close there was great excitement when it was realised that the Alfa would become the first car in the history of the race to exceed 3,000km (1,864 miles) in the 24 hours. In the event it completed 3,018.75km (1,875.8 miles), finishing 113km (70 miles) ahead of the SSK and averaging 125.7km/h (77.9mph). The Alfa 8C-2300 went on to win Le Mans for the next three years.

The year 1951 saw the dramatic beginning of a new era of one-marque dominance at Le Mans. The French were there in force, in the shape of the superb 4.5-litre Lago-Talbots; the previous year they had taken first and second place, with the winning driver, Louis Rosier, raising the lap record above 100mph (161km/h) for the first time. Rosier was back in 1951, the other works Lago-Talbot being driven by the Argentinian Froilan Gonzalez. For Italy, relative newcomers Ferrari had two 2-litre Tipo 166s driven by Louis Chiron (now over 50 years old) and Luigi Chinetti (who had won his third Le Mans two years before). Facing this formidable array of talent were three

Jaguar C-types, competition versions of the 3.4-litre, twin-cam XK 120 road car that had gained a modest 12th place at Le Mans in 1950. The drivers were Peter Walker/Peter Whitehead, Stirling Moss/Jack Fairman, and Carlo Biondetti (hero of so many Mille Miglia and Targa Florio races) partnered by Leslie Johnson.

It became clear soon after the start that the Ferraris were not 'on song' – they seemed completely outclassed. The Jaguars were clearly faster than the Lago-Talbots, but there was considerable doubt whether their greater speed would be negated, over 24 hours, by the remarkable reliability of the Talbots, which would also have to make fewer stops for refuelling.

The Moss/Fairman car was going very fast, setting record after record for the fastest lap. After four hours the three Jaguars were in the first three places, but Biondetti was soon forced to retire with no oil pressure. That left two Jaguars still in the lead, while one of the Talbots moved up to third place, only a lap behind. Then, just after midnight, a further disaster struck the Jaguar team. Stirling Moss accelerated out of a bend, and a connecting rod snapped, ruining the engine. Only the Walker/Whitehead Jaguar remained; there were 16 hours still to run, and there was speculation as to whether some inherent weakness in the XK engine had caused both the retirements. The

ABOVE Jaguar dominance at Le Mans reached its peak in 1957 when D-Types took five of the first six places. Here one of the victorious five makes a pit stop.

RIGHT This GT40 driven by Dan Gurney and Jerry Grant was pacemaker for the decisive Ford challenge at Le Mans in 1966. The winner was the Chris Amon/Bruce McLaren GT40, with the similar Ken Miles/Denny Hulme car a few metres behind.

BELOW The early 1960s were dominated by Ferrari, for whom Olivier Gendebien and American *grand-prix* driver Phil Hill formed a tremendous partnership. Here Gendebien comes through the Esses in the Ferrari 330TR/LM in 1962, when they had their third victory.

51

signal went out to the surviving car to take things as easily as possible, short of surrendering the lead. The Talbot, now in second place, was going ominously well; up into third place came an American contender – the rather overweight 5.4-litre Cunningham of John Fitch and Phil Walters.

The race was effectively decided during the night, when both the works Talbots came to grief – Rosier's with a split oil tank and Gonzalez's with a blown head gasket. The Cunningham now lay second, while the 2.6-litre Aston Martin DB2 of Lance Macklin and George Abecassis moved into third place. The Cunningham now began to slow, and a third Talbot swept past the Aston to take (and retain) second place. But the Jaguar was now safe. In spite of driving circumspectly, Walker and Whitehead won at a record average speed of 150.5km/h (93.3mph) and were more than 125km (78 miles) ahead of the Talbot.

It was certainly an auspicious occasion; but even the Jaguar team could not have anticipated the dominance the marque was to achieve at Le Mans in the next few years – especially when the C-Types were overwhelmed by the formidable Mercedes-Benz 300SL 'gull-wing' coupés in 1952. The following year the C-Types not only had more power but a decisive advantage over all their competitors in the form of disc brakes. They took first and second places, the winning car driven by Tony Rolt and Duncan Hamilton averaging 170.4km/h (105.8mph).

In 1954 Jaguar introduced the D-Type, a shorter, lighter sports-racer with a monocoque body; engine power was raised to 250bhp. After a tremendous battle, the Rolt/Hamilton yielded first place – by only about 90 seconds after 24 hours! – to the more powerful 4.9-litre V12 Ferrari 375 of Gonzalez and Maurice Trintignant. Jaguar's 1–2 victory in 1955 by Ivor Bueb and Mike Hawthorn was somewhat hollow. The D-Types were opposed by the all-conquering Mercedes-Benz 300SLRs – sports-car versions of the grand-prix W196 – piloted by such giants as Fangio and Moss. The German team, however, was withdrawn after another of its drivers, Pierre Levegh, hit an Austin-Healey on its 42nd lap and crashed into the crowd opposite the pits, killing more than 80 spectators. The following year Ron Flockart and Vivian Sanderson won in a D-Type, which now developed 300hp. But the greatest triumph of all came in 1957, when Flockart and Ivor Bueb's winning car was followed home by D-Types in second, third, fourth, and sixth places.

The early 1960s were totally dominated by Ferrari, which won all the races from 1960 to 1965, mainly with increasingly powerful versions of the marvellous 3-litre V12 Tipo 250. In 1961 and 1962 the victor for Ferrari was the formidable Phil Hill/Olivier Gendebien partnership which had also won in 1958. A portent to the future, however, was seen in 1964 when three Ford GT40 mid-engined, 4.2-litre V8 coupés entered for Le Mans; none finished but one of them, driven by Phil Hill, set a new lap record. The GT40, the result of enormous investment by American Ford, won at Le Mans in 1966 and the three following years with 7-litre engines developing 480bhp and more.

Ever since Jaguar's first successful onslaught in 1951, a small firm with a tiny fraction of Ford's resources had been sending sports cars to Le Mans and had consistently carried off awards in the 1,100 and 1,500cc classes. This was the German company Porsche run by the great Ferdinand Porsche's son, Ferry. By the mid-1960s Porsche's Le Mans contenders were looking for outright victory in the shape of the 3-litre 908, while for 1969 the marque entered the 917, with a 4.5-litre flat-12 engine developing 520bhp. Then in 1970 Porsche returned in force to Le Mans: almost half the field of 51 starters were Porsches of one kind or another. They were opposed mainly by the new 3-litre Matra-Simca prototypes, and a powerful line-up of 5-litre Ferrari 512Ss.

The race was a curious mixture – the usual process of attrition, weeding out cars one by one, interspersed with sudden disasters. Torrential rain during the night caused many accidents: a British driver, Andrew Hedges, saw a line of eight cars in front of him spin violently as they tried to brake at Mulsanne corner. The Ferrari entry was

quickly whittled away: three of the four works-entered 512s had retired after eight hours; four others, including the remaining works car, were involved later in one accident. By dawn only 28 of the original starters remained. Although privately entered Ferraris continued to prove a threat, a Porsche 917 driven by Hans Herrmann and Richard Atwood gave the marque its first outright victory. Porsche repeated its victory the following year (1971) when Helmut Marko and Gijs van Lennep's 917 recorded the highest average speed in the history of the race – 222.3km/h (138.1mph). This record is likely to stand for some time, as the circuit has since been made slower and the fastest cars – the sports prototypes – are now restricted to 3-litres capacity.

Contrary to the general impression, it is in sports cars, especially sports prototypes, rather than in *grand-prix* racers that the most significant engineering developments have been pioneered in recent years. In 1975 the 24-hour race gained greatly in excitement by the presence of Alpine-Renault's experimental 2-litre V6 prototype using a turbocharger. Porsche, too, turbocharged its old 908's 2.2-litre, air-cooled flat-six engine, winning Le Mans with it in 1976 and 1977. By 1978 Renault had got the bugs out of its turbocharged V6 and this French marque – one of the pioneers of motor sport – won Le Mans for the first time.

Meanwhile, in 1975, the Le Mans race committee had drawn up regulations that conflicted with those established by the Fédération Internationale de l'Automobile (the sport's governing body) for sports-car events. As a result, the 24-hour classic no longer forms part of the World Sports Car Championship. Most championship races today are shorter – the preferred distance is 1,000km (620 miles) – and can be completed in half a day. For the tradition-minded spectator there is still magic in the idea of a race that continues through the night, but it may be that the days of this classic event are numbered.

During the second half of the 1970s the centre of interest at Le Mans was the use of turbochargers by Renault and Porsche, which were seen first in 1975. Porsches were victorious in 1966–7, but Renault prevailed the following year. Here the Jean-Pierre Jabouille/ Patrick Depailler Renault Alpine 442 B Turbo sweeps around the Virage Ford before the pit straight in 1978. Fastest of all the cars in the race, the Jabouille Renault led until it retired during the night, victory going to the similar car of Jean-Pierre Jaussaud and Didier Pironi.

Grands Prix

However admired and respected other forms of motor sport may be, it is the *grand prix* that generates by far the greatest public enthusiasm and offers the most spectacular financial rewards to the winners. It may not be the most technically advanced form of motor sport or even the fastest – arguably, sports-car racing surpasses it on both these counts – but it is unquestionably the most glamorous: the Formula 1 championship races are mounted with all the razzmatazz of a major show-business event, and the most successful drivers enjoy the status of pop stars.

Strictly speaking the term *grand prix* applies nowadays only to the national Formula 1 events – the so-called *grandes épreuves* (great tests) – that count towards the world constructors' and drivers' championships. Today countries all over the world hold races that qualify for these championships. But for many years there was only one *grand prix* – the inspiration of the autocratic Automobile Club de France, which invented the idea. . . .

The First Grand Prix

The 1906 French Grand Prix was run over public roads that were closed to normal traffic for the duration of the race. The chosen circuit was to the east of Le Mans – a triangular route with a lap length of 103km (64 miles). The start/finish line and grandstands were at Pont-de-Gennes, a small village by the N.23 (the main Le Mans-Paris road). From there the route ran north-east on the N.23 to La Ferté-Bernard, where it turned sharp right (southward) onto the narrow D.1, passed through Vibraye Forest and came to St Calais. Here it turned westward onto the N.157, passed through Bouloire, and eventually rejoined the N.23 at a very sharp right-hand corner – the circuit's nearest point to Le Mans.

Today the route makes a comfortable morning's drive. In 1906, however, the road surfaces were gravel and dirt. The minor road through the forest was scarcely more than a cart track, and long sections of it had to be laid with wooden planks, which were also used to make a by-pass around St Calais. Elsewhere the D.1 and part of the N.157 were sprayed with tar to hold the gravel surface together. The race was run over two consecutive days in June, with six laps of the circuit on each day – a total distance of 1,236km (768 miles), which is exceptionally long by modern standards. There was no mass start, as in modern *grands prix*: the cars were despatched at intervals of 90 seconds. Replacement drivers would be allowed for the second day.

The only regulation governing the size of the cars was a maximum weight limit of 1,000kg (just under a ton). Given a very light two-seater body, this meant the machinery beneath could be big and heavy. All the engines had four cylinders, but the capacities varied greatly. The smallest engine, in a Grégoire, was of 8 litres; those in the Richard-Brasiers and Renaults were of almost 13 litres; that of the Vulpes was 15.2 litres; while those of the Panhards and FIATs (the name was spelled in capitals until 1908) were of no less than 18 litres. All the cars had feeble brakes operating only on the rear wheels; some had three gears, others four; some put their faith in chain drive, others in the more advanced shaft drive. The biggest technical debate focused on wheels and tyres. A very fast, long-distance race along indifferent roads was going to be extremely hard on tyres, yet the race regulations allowed only the driver and his riding mechanic to work on the cars in case of breakdown. In the early days of the century, changeable wheels with ready-mounted tyres were unknown. If a tyre punctured, it had to be removed from the wheel (often it was cut off with jack-knives) and a new tyre and inner tube fitted and pumped up. Racing crews were expert at this (one authority claims that two good men could carry out a change in five minutes, although a quarter of an hour must have been more usual); in a race, however, even five minutes is a lot of time to make up. For the 1906 race the tyre manufacturer André Michelin offered an ingenious solution to the problem – a wheel with a detachable rim to which a tyre was fitted, the idea being to carry a set of spare, tyred rims. It promised to cut in half the time taken to get under

way again after suffering a puncture. Renault, Itala, and FIAT decided to use it; the other teams did not, arguing that the extra weight of the spare rims would slow the cars and might, indeed, increase the rate of tyre failure.

The summer of 1906 was extremely hot, and on the day of the race the temperature was as high as many people could remember. This was bad news all round: the race would be a terrible test of stamina for the drivers; the cars, with their crude cooling systems (some did not even have water pumps), were likely to overheat and boil over frequently; and the newly sprayed tar on the roads would melt.

The drivers assembled for the start at 06.00hrs. Many were already heroes to motor-racing enthusiasts: Fernand Gabriel, Louis Wagner, and Victor Hémery of France, Camille Jenatzy of Belgium, and Felice Nazzaro and Vincenzo Lancia of Italy (the last was in 1908 to begin building the cars that still bear his name). There was also Ferenc Szisz, a Hungarian test engineer for Renault, who had been Louis Renault's driving mechanic in the catastrophic Paris–Madrid race three years before.

The first to be flagged away was Gabriel in his 17.2-litre De Diétrich; the starting interval meant it was over three-quarters of an hour before the final competitor, Touloubre in the third of the Clément-Bayards, set off in pursuit. After that, the crowds in the grandstands had only a few minutes to wait before the early starters completed the first lap. Gabriel had gone missing, and the first man through was Lancia in the big FIAT, hotly pursued by Szisz in his Renault. Then came the Richard-Brasier of Fernand Baras, whose first lap was the fastest of all. In spite of the poor roads and the primitive design of the cars, the speeds were remarkably high: Baras' lap time represented an average speed of 118km/h (73mph); and Szisz was timed through a flying kilometre at nearly 149km/h (92.4mph).

It was not long before the conditions began to take their toll, and Renault's wisdom in using the Michelin detachable rim became evident. Baras

put in one more very fast lap, but then ran into tyre trouble and never again completed a lap in under an hour except once on the second day.

As the morning wore on, the stones on the road, each wrapped in an envelope of molten tar, began to bother the drivers. The worst sufferer was Edmond in the second of the works Renaults; a stone smashed his goggles, and glass splinters and drops of tar entered his eye. The regulations forbade his replacement by another driver on the first day, so he struggled on until he was overcome by pain and was forced to retire. (Jenatzy and Lancia also suffered with tar in their eyes, and at the end of the first day the official doctor ordered them to hand over their cars to the reserve drivers. Lancia could not or would not understand the doctor's French: he took his car out again the following day – only to retire when his FIAT suffered mechanical failure.)

There were many crashes, most of them caused by punctures or wheel failures as the cars pounded along the atrocious roads. Heroic feats of rebuilding were carried out, and a special cheer went up for Le Blon, who finally reappeared after taking over four hours to complete a single lap in his wounded Hotchkiss. By this time Szisz was well on the way to completing his first day's task, and at 11.49 he crossed the line at the conclusion of his sixth lap – the only one on which he had taken

more than one hour. Albert Clément, in one of his father's 12.8-litre Clément-Bayards, was second, 26 minutes behind, while Nazzaro, FIAT's number one driver, was a further 15 minutes in arrears. After that it was a question of waiting to see what happened to the stragglers, but to all intents and purposes the first day was over by lunch time. Only 17 of the original 32 cars remained to carry on the next day.

There was no stopping Szisz, who sensibly eased off once he realised how much time he had in hand, and contented himself with lapping between five and 10 minutes slower than on the previous day. Only on the third lap did he speed up to anything like his original place, apparently in response to a fast second lap by Clément; but he still managed a race average of over 101km/h (63mph). Meanwhile a tremendous battle was developing for second place between Clément and Nazzaro, which came to a head when the Italian slashed almost 20 minutes off Clément's lead on the third lap. However, Nazzaro had his own problems, for on the following lap his massive FIAT broke a rear spring, which did nothing for its already dubious handling. He pressed on bravely, however, and eventually finished over half an hour behind Szisz but some three minutes ahead of Clément. These were the only three drivers to complete the full 12 laps. There were

RIGHT Newcomer Christian Läutenschlager making one of no less than 11 tyre changes in the 1908 French Grand Prix at Dieppe. In spite of such hold-ups he took his 12.8-litre, four-cylinder Mercedes 120PS to victory, averaging 111.3km/h (69.1mph).

BELOW RIGHT French ace Georges Boillot in the 1913 French Grand Prix at Amiens – his second successive win. His advanced 7.6-litre Peugeot humbled its larger-engined rivals.

BELOW Map of the 1906 French Grand Prix circuit east of Le Mans. The race, run over two days, consisted of 12 laps of 103km (64 miles). The smaller circuit, at left, is that used for the Le Mans 24-hour race.

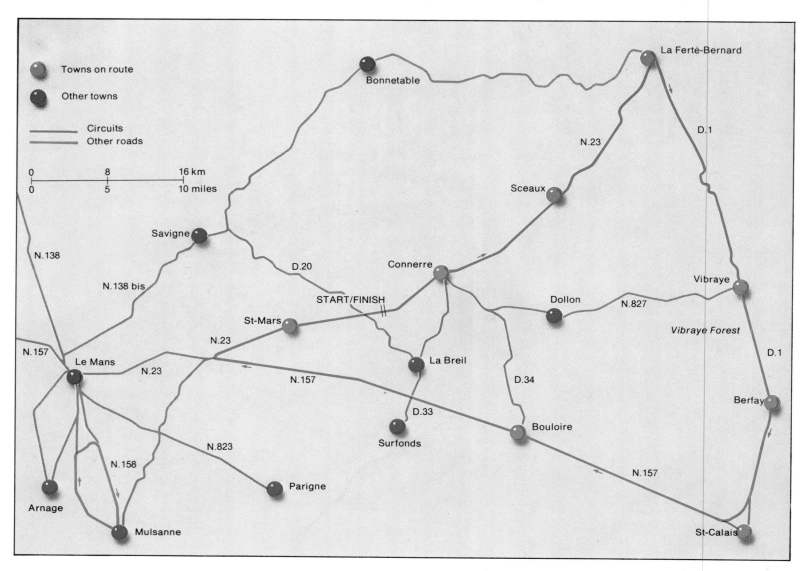

La Ferté-Bernard

Bonnetable

Towns on route

Other towns

Circuits
Other roads

D.1

N.23

0   8   16 km
0   5   10 miles

Sceaux

Savigne

D.20   Connerre

N.138

Vibraye

N.138 bis

START/FINISH   Dollon   N.827

St-Mars   Vibraye Forest

N.23

D.1

N.157   N.23   La Breil

Le Mans   N.23   D.34

N.157

Berfay

D.33

N.823   Bouloire

Surfonds

N.158   Parigne   N.157

Arnage

Mulsanne   St-Calais

great scenes of triumph when Szisz arrived at the finish, and Louis Renault and his driver were embraced by the French Minister of Commerce: a French car had won France's premier event, and that was the important thing.

Many lessons were learned in that first *grand prix*. The most valuable technical conclusion was that the biggest-engined cars were not always the fastest, for the winning Renault had the smallest engine of the serious contenders in the 1906 race. It was also clear that advances were needed in wheel and tyre design. The correspondent of the *Autocar* wrote of the race that it was 'one of men, luck, and tyres, chiefly tyres'.

As to organisation, it was obvious that a two-day event on an enormous circuit posed unnecessary problems of control and communication, to say nothing of keeping the spectators interested. All future *grands prix* (except for the 1912 event) would be run in a single day, and the circuits gradually became shorter. Different formulas governing total weight and engine capacity would also be tried in order to make the racing more competitive. Nazzaro came to Dieppe in 1907 to win the second *grand prix* for FIAT, beating Szisz into second place. In 1908 the event returned to Dieppe and this time it was Mercedes that won – a remarkable triumph for Christian Läutenschlager, Mercedes' chief car-tester, who was taking part in his first major race. The 1908 event was a humbling experience for the host nation, six of the first seven cars to finish being Mercedes or Benz racers, the highest French placing being fourth.

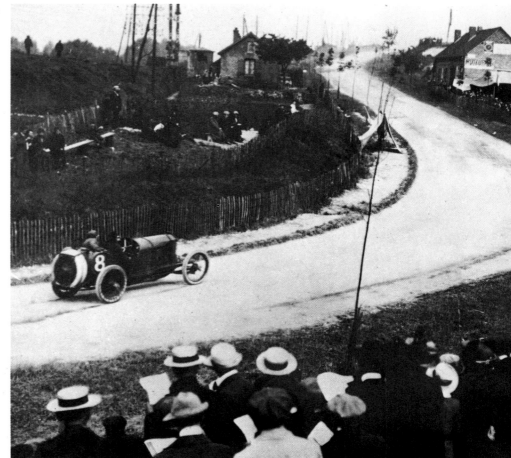

The 1914 Grand Prix

After two foreign wins in a row, French enthusiasm waned slightly and the next true *grand prix* did not take place until 1912, when Georges Boillot restored French pride with a win in his Peugeot at Dieppe; and he repeated this triumph the following year at Amiens. The French indeed, were vehemently chauvinistic in their attitude toward the *grand prix*: they regarded it as *their* race, and hated to see victory going to foreign cars. It is easy to imagine the emotional frenzy of the crowd at the 1914 *grand prix* (at Lyons), which was run only four weeks before the outbreak of World War I. It was, in fact, one of the most significant *grands prix* in history. Technically it proved to be a contest between what were then the two most advanced marques in the world – Peugeot of France and Mercedes of Germany. The 4.5-litre Peugeot engine, developed by the brilliant Swiss engineer Ernest Henri, can be regarded as the ancestor of the modern high-performance car engine; it used twin overhead camshafts to operate four valves per cylinder, and developed 112bhp at the then high speed of 2,900rpm. To improve cornering performance the Peugeots were fitted with brakes on all four wheels (the first time the system was used in a *grand prix*). Henri's opposite number in the Mercedes camp was Paul Daimler (son of the car pioneer). His cars also had engines of 4.5 litres (the maximum capacity permitted by the ACF for this race), with single overhead camshafts, and four valves and three sparking plugs per cylinder; they developed 115bhp at 3,200rpm. Both the Peugeot and the Mercedes developed more power at more readily usable engine speeds than the vast, heavy, slow-revving cars of earlier days, and they had far better handling and road-holding.

If the contending cars were evenly matched, the Germans proved masters of team tactics (the race, incidentally, was the first in which pit signals were used on a large scale). The German plan was for one of the Mercedes drivers, Max Sailer, to push

ABOVE Louis Wagner (Mercedes) on the back leg of the Givors circuit, near Lyons, during the epic French Grand Prix of 1914. Wagner took second place.

Christian Läutenschlager (Mercedes), the winner, comes out of the hairpin on the famed 'Deathtrap' section of the Givors circuit. He finally put paid to Georges Boillot's chances on the 18th lap.

his car to its limit from the start, in the confident expectation that the brilliant but vainglorious Georges Boillot would chase him and overtax his Peugeot rather than bide his time. Then the rest of the Mercedes team would pick off the ailing Peugeots of Boillot and his team-mate, Jules Goux, towards the end of the race. And that is exactly what happened. Sailer was 1½ minutes ahead of Boillot by the end of the third lap of the 37.5km (23.3-mile) circuit; on the fourth lap he broke the circuit record – and then one of his connecting rods snapped. He was out of the race, but his job was done. By now Christian Läutenschlager in the second Mercedes was beginning to press Boillot, who immediately stepped up his speed. But the Mercedes challenge was remorseless: by lap 17 (with only three to go) Läutenschlager had cut Boillot's lead to 14 seconds, and on the 18th he passed him; by now the Peugeot was sick, and on the next lap it threw a valve. The Mercedes team of Läutenschlager, Louis Wagner, and Otto Salzer recorded the first-ever 1-2-3 grand-prix victory, Goux's Peugeot limping in in fourth place. The vast French crowd was stunned – and the official band was unable to play the German national anthem because it had 'mislaid' the music.

The post-World War I *grands prix* got under way with the 1921 event on what was to become the Le Mans 24-hour race circuit. Wartime aero-engine technology had made the four-cylinder *grand-prix* engine obsolete and six- and eight-cylinder racers began to dominate. The 1921 race was run to the Indianapolis 3-litre formula and, appropriately, was won by the American Jimmy Murphy in a straight-eight Duesenberg fitted with hydraulic brakes. Henceforward other European countries were to stage *grandes épreuves*. Italy's first, in 1921, was at Brescia (thereafter, however, it was at Monza); in 1925 the first Belgian Grand Prix was held, and the following year the British and Germans followed suit. The formulas adopted during the 1920s varied widely: 2 litres maximum in 1922–5 (in the last of those years the riding mechanic was banned); 1.5 litres maximum in 1926–7; and no capacity restrictions in 1928–33. This period saw the introduction of superchargers in *grand-prix* racers – in 1923 on the eight-cylinder Fiat 805; in 1924 on the 2-litre Alfa Romeo P2 designed by Vittorio Jano, who had just been lured away from Fiat; in 1926 on the 1.5-litre (later 2- and 2.3-litre) Bugatti Type 35; in 1927 on the 1.5-litre, straight-eight Delage 15-S8.

1935 German Grand Prix

In 1934 the *formula libre* (no-capacity-limit) regulation was replaced by a maximum weight limit of 750kg (1,653.5lb – about two thirds of a ton). This year saw the rise of the great Mercedes-Benz and Auto Union racers (backed with massive funds from Hitler's government) that were to dominate the European *grands prix* until World War II. The first of these new Mercedes racers was the W25, a supercharged straight-eight of 3.4-litres developing 314bhp. Auto Union came up with the P-Wagen (named after Ferdinand Porsche, its designer), with a supercharged V16 engine of 4.3 litres mounted at the rear. Both cars had independent suspension all-round – a major advance. The two marques had an indifferent 1934 season; but during the following winter Porsche and Mercedes-Benz's designer Dr Hans Niebel transformed the reliability of their silver monsters (Mercedes was, in fact, going to win nine of the major European races in 1935).

A vast crowd assembled at the Nürburgring (south of Bonn) for the German Grand Prix of 1935; they had every reason to believe that the racers of the Fatherland were about to humiliate the opposition. The race was 22 laps of the 22.8km (14.2-mile) circuit – a distance of 502km (312 miles).

The Mercedes-Benz team was running the W25C, now bored out to 4.3 litres and developing 462bhp at 5,800rpm. The team drivers were the great Rudolf Caracciola, the Italian ace Luigi Fagioli, the arrogant Prussian Manfred von Brauchitsch, the ex-mechanic Hermann Lang, and

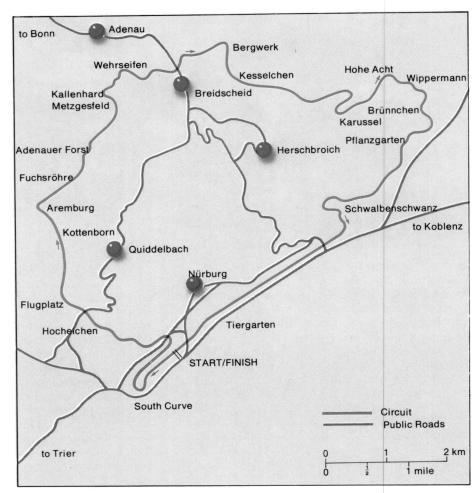

ABOVE Map of the Nürburgring, near Bonn.

LEFT German Grand Prix 1935: Tazio Nuvolari fumes while his pit mechanics struggle to refuel his Alfa Romeo P3. The delay, caused by a blocked fuel pump (the petrol had to be poured by hand), cost the Italian maestro the lead, but he went on to win in the greatest performance of his long career.

RIGHT Richard Seaman (Mercedes-Benz) chases Bernd Rosemeyer (Auto Union) on his way to victory in the German Grand Prix of 1938. German cars totally dominated *grands prix* in the late 1930s. Seaman's W154 (an early version of the W163) had a 3-litre V12 engine with two-stage supercharger and developed 465bhp. Rosemeyer's D-type also had a 3-litre V12 unit but with a single-stage supercharger; its cockpit was farther back than on earlier Auto Unions.

Designer Vittorio Jano's masterpiece, the Alfa Romeo Tipo B, known popularly as the P3, made its debut in 1932 and swiftly created a legendary reputation. Originally of 2.7 litres, its supercharged straight-eight engine was bored out progressively to 3.8 litres maximum.

Hans Greier. Auto Union was fielding Type B racers of 4.9 litres, driven by Bernd Rosemeyer, Achille Varzi (who had recently joined Auto Union from Alfa Romeo), the hill-climb master Hans Stuck, and Paul Pietsch.

The opposition consisted mainly of three brilliant drivers in what appeared to be sadly outclassed Alfa Romeo P3s: the incomparable Tazio Nuvolari, the stylish French maestro Louis Chiron, and the young Italian aristocrat Antonio Brivio. Chiron's and Brivio's P3s had 3.5-litre straight-eights, while Nuvolari's had a 3.8-litre straight-eight developing 300bhp. The Alfas had inferior acceleration to the German cars and a top speed of at least 30km/h (19mph) less than the Mercedes'. Their only hope lay in the Alfa's wonderful agility, which might give it some advantage on the fast but undulating and many-cornered circuit. The rest of the field was made up of 3.7- and 2.9-litre Maseratis, a 4.9-litre Bugatti Type 59 (driven by Piero Taruffi), and Raymond Mays' British 2-litre ERA – all hopelessly outclassed in this company.

The start of the race was notable in that it anticipated modern practice by using a traffic-light system rather than a man with a flag. The 20 cars – a big *grand-prix* field for those days – rushed towards the South Curve in a shower of spray. As they returned on the far side of the pits it was Caracciola's Mercedes in the lead, and behind him a great duel was going on between Fagioli's Mercedes and Nuvolari's Alfa. Manfred von Brauchitsch had his Mercedes in fourth place, while Raymond Mays was holding a highly creditable fifth with the ERA. The Auto Unions had had a bad start and all lay well back in the field.

The first-lap Caracciola-Nuvolari duel showed the different characteristics of their cars. The Mercedes gained on the fast downhill corners to Flugplatz (aerodrome), the Bergwerk-Karussel-Hohe Acht section on the north side of the circuit, and on the long, undulating straight back to the pits. The Alfa hauled it back on the tricky corners after Fuchsröhre (Fox Throat) and the difficult sections from the bridge at Brünnchen through Schwalbenschwanz (Swallowtail) before the home straight. Caracciola led Nuvolari by 12 seconds at the end of the first lap. Nuvolari then seemed to coast for a few laps: he was passed by Rosemeyer, Brauchitsch, and Fagioli. Brivio's Alfa Romeo had already dropped out with differential trouble; then on the fourth lap Nuvolari's other team-mate, Chiron, retired for the same reason. On lap 5 Rosemeyer lost ground again, the Auto Union's engine beginning to sound sick.

Nuvolari made his next move on lap 6, passing both Rosemeyer and Brauchitsch. With Fagioli calling at the pits, Nuvolari was now in second place, in pursuit of the flying Caracciola. To the astonishment of the crowd, he was first past the pits at the end of the 10th lap; he was closely followed by a resurgent Rosemeyer, Brauchitsch, and Caracciola, who had suddenly dropped down the field.

At the end of lap 12 the four leaders stopped at the pits to refuel and change tyres. Here German efficiency completely transformed the order of the race. Brauchitsch's crew got him away in under 50 seconds; Caracciola followed a few seconds later, and Rosemeyer was off in 1 minute 15 seconds. Nuvolari's crew took a disastrous 2 minutes 15 seconds, and the Alfa rejoined the race in sixth place.

How could any driver survive such a crushing blow to his morale? Nuvolari had driven like one possessed to gain that lead. Yet his misfortune seemed only to act as a spur, and he set off once again in pursuit of his German adversaries. Those who witnessed that drive say there has never been anything to equal it. By the end of the 13th lap Nuvolari had passed Rosemeyer, Caracciola, Fagioli, and Stuck; but even the most hopeful arithmetic suggested that Brauchitsch – with a lead of more than 1 minute 25 seconds out of the pits – was beyond all catching. Indeed, Brauchitsch responded to Nuvolari's threat with a new lap record of $10\frac{1}{2}$ minutes, adding 16 seconds to his dwindling lead.

Then fate took a final hand, proving as kind to

Nuvolari as his pit stop had been unkind. With two laps remaining, Brauchitsch's right front tyre had virtually worn away its tread. He could not afford to slow because Nuvolari had whittled his lead down to 32 seconds. On the final lap, only 8km (5 miles) from the finish Brauchitsch's tyre blew. Nuvolari shot past him, to win the race of his life. He was followed home by Stuck, with Caracciola the best placed of the Mercedes team in third place, Rosemeyer fourth, and the unlucky Brauchitsch taking fifth place on three tyres and a wheel rim.

The race was a crushing blow to German pride, but even the most nationalistic spectators admitted that they had seen one of the greatest races in history. Besides, the more knowledgeable among them knew that the success of the brilliant design teams at Mercedes-Benz and Auto Union could not long be denied.

Indeed, so overwhelmingly successful were the German cars during the next two seasons that the French and Italians concentrated thereafter on what was known as the *voiturette* class, in which engine capacities were limited to 1.5 litres. The most significant outcome of this development was the classic Alfa Romeo Tipo 158, designed by Gioacchino Colombo. It was not only enormously successful before the war: it dominated *grand-prix* racing in the immediately post-war years, when the championship was renewed on the basis of the 1.5-litre formula. Giuseppe Farina (once Nuvolari's protégé) in 1950 and Juan Manuel Fangio in 1951 became world champions driving the 158 and its successor, the 159, which was fitted with a two-stage supercharger and developed a remarkable 420bhp.

Alfa Romeo gave up *grand-prix* racing after 1951. The way was now open for the first period of Ferrari dominance. The formula was changed to 2 litres, unsupercharged, and Ferrari's number-one driver, Alberto Ascari, took the championship in 1952 and 1953. Ascari, indeed, proved almost unbeatable at this time, and in many 1953 races the greatest excitement was generated by the duels fought out between Fangio (by then 42 years old), driving a Maserati, and the 24-year-old

In the 1953 French Grand Prix at Rheims, one of the epic races of that season, Mike Hawthorn beat Juan Manuel Fangio by about one second to record his first-ever championship win. Here Fangio (Maserati A6SSG) fights off a challenge by Hawthorn (Ferrari Tipo 500) during the race.

Mike Hawthorn (Ferrari), then in his second season of *grand-prix* racing.

Hawthorn had beaten Fangio by a whisker to win the French Grand Prix at Rheims. Their next close encounter was in the German Grand Prix at the Nürburgring. The line-up included the Ferrari Tipo 500s of Ascari, Farina, Luigi Villoresi, and Hawthorn; the Maserati A6SSGs of Fangio and his fellow Argentinian, Froilan Gonzalez; a pair of fast but fragile Gordinis from France; and a clutch of assorted hardware from Britain – Connaughts, a Cooper-Bristol, a Veritas, and a Cooper-Alta driven by the young Stirling Moss.

The start was tremendous, and there was an immediate scramble for the lead, with Fangio in front going into the South Curve but Ascari over-taking him on the exit, the pair of them closely pursued by Hawthorn. By the end of the first lap Ascari was well in front, but Hawthorn was snapping at the heels of Fangio's Maserati. Even as the crowd in the grandstand watched, the pair changed places twice, and it was clear that the Ferrari was quicker through the corners and the Maserati was faster along the straights.

The first shock came on lap 5, when Ascari limped into the pits on three wheels and a front brake drum. He overshot the pits, and his mechanics had to chase after him with a jack so that he could replace the lost wheel before reversing to his team's pit position. Many minutes were lost, and for once Ascari was out of the running. His loss seemed to stimulate his team-mate Farina, who was reputed to be unhappy about his role as the Ferrari team's number-two driver behind Ascari. Suddenly Farina began to go much more quickly, reeling in Hawthorn and Fangio to pass them on the eighth lap. A long way behind him, Ascari

restarted, pulled into the pits once again, and set off in pursuit of the leaders.

Small though the field had been, retirements were taking their toll. The Gordinis and all but one of the Connaughts dropped out with various problems, but most of the attention was by this time on the flying Farina in the lead, and on the battle being waged by Ascari to catch the duelling Hawthorn and Fangio. It was a duel which seemed likely to be resolved in Fangio's favour, for he pulled slowly away from the British driver, leaving him as a target for Ascari.

Once again it was not to be. The normally reliable Ferrari let down the champion, still in fourth place although closing on Hawthorn: Ascari's engine blew up as he passed the back of the pits coming down from the South Curve. Nor was the drama yet over, except for Farina who looked increasingly safe up ahead. Fangio's car shed its exhaust; and this, apart from its effect on performance, allowed fumes and heat to be swept back along the car to its driver. Fangio, a stronger and much more determined man than most, slowed but not enough to surrender second place.

Farina's winning speed was fractionally better than that recorded by Ascari in 1951 (in a sup-posedly much more powerful Formula 1 car), and he was over a minute ahead of Fangio at the end. The Argentinian in turn was over half a minute ahead of Hawthorn, even though he had been half-cooked in the process. Stirling Moss was sixth after a difficult drive with gear-selection problems in the Cooper-Alta.

Over the next dozen years the formula changed twice: 2.5 litres for 1954–60 and 1.5 litres for 1961–5. The banning of superchargers for these small engines meant that the cars were unexciting in terms of sheer speed and acceleration. But this had the salutary effect of forcing developments to improve handling, cornering, and braking. The disc brake, as we have seen, was pioneered by Jaguar in 1953 and it was soon to be used on *grand-prix* cars. The 1954–5, 2.5-litre formula was dominated by Mercedes-Benz: the fuel-injected W196 *grand-prix* car proved almost as unbeatable as did the related 300SLR in the sports-car field; it developed 310bhp at 8,000rpm, was capable of 300km/h (186mph), and gave Fangio his second and third world titles – in 1955 hotly pursued by Stirling Moss, who had also joined the Stuttgart stable. Mercedes might well have gone on to further triumphs; but the terrible crash of Pierre Levegh's 300SLR at Le Mans in 1955 led to the factory's withdrawal from all forms of racing.

By the mid-1950s Britain had four young drivers of exceptional talent in Moss, Hawthorn, Peter Collins, and Tony Brooks. In 1958, after four years

of steady improvement, Britain won the world constructors' championship for the first time in the shape of the Vanwall, a four-cylinder racer partly designed by Lotus chief Colin Chapman. British teams had, indeed, arrived: they pioneered the post-war mid-engined *grand-prix* car (with the engine behind the driver), and in 1959 they took the constructors' championship again with the Cooper, powered by the Coventry-Climax engine and driven by Jack Brabham – a victory repeated the following year.

In the first half of the 1960s the *grand-prix* scene was hardly improved by the 1.5-litre unsupercharged capacity limit for Formula 1 cars, but it saw the emergence and triumph of what turned out to be the virtually unbeatable combination of Jim Clark and Colin Chapman's Lotus 25. The bodywork of the car was so designed that Clark sat in an almost prone position and had to adopt a straight-armed steering style. It all seemed biz-

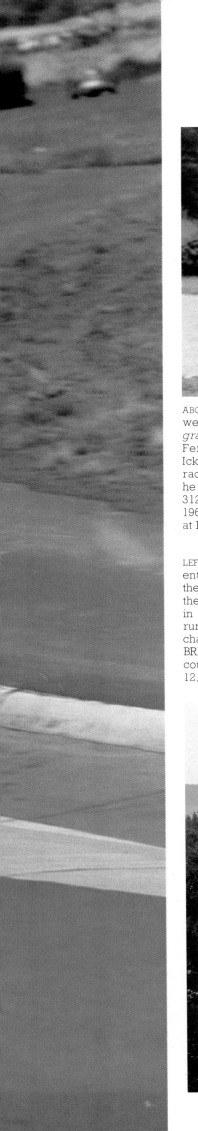

ABOVE The late 1960s were an indifferent *grand-prix* period for Ferrari, although Jacky Ickx drove some brilliant races for the team. Here he takes a Ferrari Tipo 312 to victory in the 1968 French Grand Prix at Rouen.

LEFT Graham Hill (BRM) enters the Karussel on the Nürburgring during the German Grand Prix in 1965, when he was runner-up in the drivers' championship. The BRM's 1.5-litre engine could turn at almost 12,000rpm.

arre at the time – but it is now commonplace on almost all Formula 1 cars. Clark won seven out of the 10 *grands prix* in 1963 and waltzed away with the title with the maximum number of possible points (the seven best results of each driver counting towards the championship). In 1966 the Formula 1 regulations changed again, this time to the 3-litre unsupercharged/1.5-litre supercharged maximums that have continued, with minor modifications, to the present day. This was the year, too, in which Colin Chapman signed a large sponsorship agreement not with one of the oil or tyre companies – then the major sponsors of Formula 1 racing – but with a cigarette manufacturer. British 'racing green', the traditional colour of British *grand-prix* cars, gave way on the Lotus racers to the red and gold of Player's Gold Leaf, and within a few years sponsors' colours, rather than national colours, would appear on most *grand-prix* racers.

BELOW The climb up to the famous banked Karussel of the Nürburgring in the 1972 German Grand Prix. The hilly, many-cornered Ring, overlooked by Nürburg castle, was by then causing anxiety among the increasingly safety-conscious *grand-prix* drivers. Since the accident that almost killed Niki Lauda in the 1976 race, the German Grand Prix has been held at Hockenheim, near Heidelberg, but there are plans to build a shorter, safer circuit to replace the old one at Nürburg.

The 1969 Monaco Grand Prix

The 3-litre formula had been introduced at the last moment and at first took some constructors by surprise, but eventually it led to much faster cars. The new kind of racing was seen at its best in such races as the Monaco Grand Prix of 1969. Monaco is a unique event – a genuine 'around the houses' race, the route passing the famous Monte Carlo Casino, the luxury hotels, and promenades on two sides of the harbour. The constant twists and turns – in 1969 there were 80 laps of the 3km (1.9-mile) circuit – are a formidable test for car and driver. That year the Monaco had a special flavour: the racing world wanted to see if Graham Hill (Lotus 49B) could win the race for a record fifth time. Hill's main rivals were Jackie Stewart (Matra MS80), who was to win his first drivers' world championship that year; Jean-Pierre Beltoise in the second Matra; Chris Amon in a Ferrari T312; and Piers Courage (who was to die later in the season in the Dutch Grand Prix) in a Brabham BT26. Hill's chances were reckoned to be slim after the pre-race practice sessions had put him on the second row of the starting grid behind Stewart, Amon, and Beltoise. On most other *grand-prix* circuits the second row is quite a reasonable position. At Monaco, however, the leader has an enormous advantage, even over potentially faster cars, because the serpentine nature of the course offers so few opportunities for overtaking.

From the start Stewart and Amon quickly established a lead over Beltoise and Hill. The race took a heavy toll of cars almost from the first lap. By the 20th lap, accidents and failures had reduced the field to only eight cars. Amon was the first of the front-runners to retire, the gearbox of the Ferrari giving up on lap 17. Then, within the space of two laps, both Stewart's and Beltoise's Matras broke their drive shafts. Hill, who had been in second place but some way behind Stewart, inherited the lead. Courage now moved into second place, steadily gaining on Hill with almost every lap that passed. But Hill was a master at Monaco. The circuit has almost invariably taken a heavy mechanical toll of cars, yet Hill seemed always to know exactly how much he could ask of his machinery there. So it was in 1969. He calculated to a nicety what he had to do in terms of fending off Courage's challenge while pushing the Lotus no harder than was absolutely necessary. He was rewarded with his fifth win at Monaco – one of the most popular victories in the circuit's history.

ABOVE LEFT Map of the Monaco circuit, which winds for 3.3km (2.1 miles) through the streets of Monte Carlo. It is the slowest of the championship circuits, the main problem for drivers being the difficulty of overtaking.

RIGHT During the 1960s Graham Hill was supreme at Monaco, winning five times in 1963–9 – three in a row for BRM and twice for

Lotus. Here he is on his way to his final victory in the Lotus 49B.

ABOVE RIGHT Hill's main rival in the 1969 race was Jackie Stewart in the Ken Tyrell Matra-Ford MS80, seen here in practice before the race (the high wing mounted on the rear suspension was banned from the race proper). Stewart retired early at Monaco but won the drivers' title later that year.

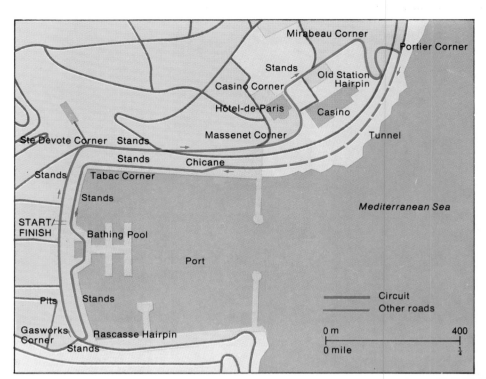

Today's Grand Prix Cars

Over the past two decades major advances in *grand-prix* car design have occurred in four main areas: tyres, chassis, aerodynamics, and engines. Tyres have altered most notably in width, the maximum wheel width now permitted – 553.4mm (21in) – leading to the use of extremely wide rear tyres. Nowadays it is usual to have the front and rear tyres made of different rubber compounds in order to improve the handling; indeed, the compound on each of the front wheels may be different because the front left tyre is subjected to greater loads and heavier wear (all circuits being run in a clockwise direction). Different types of tyre are also used in wet and dry conditions; if a downpour of rain occurs during a hitherto 'dry' race, the organisers will usually call a temporary halt to allow 'wet' tyres with greater grip to be fitted. Finally, teams nowadays usually fit 'sticky' (specially soft) tyres for the pre-race practices. These tyres last only for a few laps, but during that time they offer much better adhesion than normal race tyres – and so give drivers a chance of securing a better position on the starting grid.

Although the most obvious change in chassis design has been the re-positioning of the engine at the rear of the car (strictly, a 'mid-engine' location, since the engine is basically forward of the rear wheels), equally important has been the adoption of the monocoque principle. In its most developed form this does away with a chassis in favour of a load-bearing body consisting of 'boxes' of riveted aluminium sheet strengthened laterally at various points along the hull. In such bodies even the engine acts as a stressed 'chassis' member: it is bolted directly onto the rearmost box, with the rear suspension members attached to the engine casing or to the axle.

The aerodynamics of *grand-prix* cars is now a very sophisticated art. The problem is not merely the obvious one of making a car's shape as 'slippery' as possible, in order to reduce air resistance. Just as important is to devise means whereby the air tends to press the car downwards, so improving its adhesion to the road. Front-end spoilers and 'wings' and rear-end aerofoils all tend to have this effect, acting rather like an inverted aeroplane wing. The latest cars use a variety of methods – including flexible 'skirts' that rub along the road surface – to deflect air from the underside of the car.

Since 1967 – a year after the introduction of the 3-litre formula – the single most successful *grand-prix* engine has been the Ford DFV V8 unit designed and manufactured by Cosworth Engineering of Northampton. Although originally exclusive to Lotus cars, it has been used by many other racing teams including, notably the Matra in which Jackie Stewart won his first world championship in 1969, the Tyrell in which he gained his second in 1971, and the McLarens that won Emerson Fittipaldi the title in 1974 and James Hunt the title in 1976. Ferrari, of course, has always built its own engines – a series of outstanding flat-12s that, in recent years, have won the title for Niki Lauda (1975 and 1977) and Jody Scheckter (1979). Other constructors to have built their own engines include Alfa Romeo, whose flat-12s were used by

OPPOSITE PAGE The unsupercharged-3-litre formula of 1966 onward allowed the alternative of supercharged engines of up to 1.5 litres. Renault was first to triumph with this option, Jean-Pierre Jabouille winning the 1979 French Grand Prix in a turbocharged car.

LEFT The Lotus 78, seen here with the late Ronnie Peterson at the wheel, pioneered 'ground-effect' aerodynamics. The car brought Peterson's team-mate, the brilliant American all-rounder Mario Andretti, the driver's world championship in 1978.

BELOW The Cosworth-Ford V8 was the most successful *grand-prix* engine of the 1970s. In this Lotus 49 (as in other monocoque racers) it acted as a stressed member of the structure, and the lower arm of the rear suspension was bolted onto the casing.

the Brabham team in the late 1970s; and the Chrysler-owned Matra, whose V12 engine has powered the successful Ligier.

Since 1977 the most interesting development in engines has been the 1.5-litre turbocharged V6 with which Renault has returned to *grand-prix* racing after a long absence. Whereas a supercharger must be mechanically powered, a turbocharger's compressor is driven by the exhaust gases; it increases an engine's output by more than one third by forcing gas into the cylinders. Renault pioneered the use of turbochargers in its 2-litre Le Mans cars in 1975 (as also did Porsche in that year's race). For 1979 Renault's *grand-prix* car used a turbocharger with two tiny turbine units instead of one. The marque crowned a period of prodigious investment when Jean-Pierre Jabouille won the French Grand Prix. The wheel had at last turned full circle: it was Renault's first *grand-prix* victory since Ferenc Szisz's historic triumph 73 years before.

RIGHT For the *grand prix* the streets of Monaco are lined with several kilometres of Armco protective barrier. In this shot of the 1979 race Jody Scheckter (Ferrari) leads Patrick Depailler (Ligier), Gilles Villeneuve (Ferrari), and Niki Lauda (Brabham). Scheckter won, and went on to clinch the 1979 drivers' title.

ABOVE Driver-safety regulations have steadily improved in recent years. Niki Lauda's gear included an all-enveloping helmet over a fire-resistant face-mask, and a fresh-air pipe to enable him to breathe freely in event of a fire.

LEFT Lauda's great years were the mid-1970s, when he was often unbeatable in the superb flat-12 Ferraris. He took the drivers' title in 1975 (here he is winning at Monaco that year) and 1977. He retired during the 1979 season.

Great Drivers

The question of who was the greatest racing driver of all time provokes strenuous argument but no satisfactory answer – too many imponderables and provisos confuse the issue. For example, it is pointless to make judgments on the basis of the number of victories achieved: there have been fewer *grands prix* in some periods than in others. Moreover, the relative quality of the cars available in given seasons has often favoured some drivers at the expense of other, perhaps more gifted ones. Some drivers have refused at various times to advance their careers in foreign cars on grounds of patriotism; others seem to have been dogged by bad luck (as opposed to bad judgment) in their choice of marques. Above all, the evolution of *grand-prix* and sports-racing cars over the past 70 years has called for different driving qualities and techniques. In earlier times the top drivers could force cars to their mechanical limits without overtaxing their own skills; today the performance of the fastest cars is so great that even the finest drivers cannot exploit it to the full except for a few seconds at a time. This does not mean that the present generation of drivers is inferior to those of the past – merely that it has to be assessed in different ways.

Nevertheless, the 14 racing drivers whose careers are outlined on the following pages would all feature in most people's list of the 20 greatest. Some were undoubtedly better than the others. Here they appear in order of their dates of birth: placing them in order of greatness is up to the reader. . . .

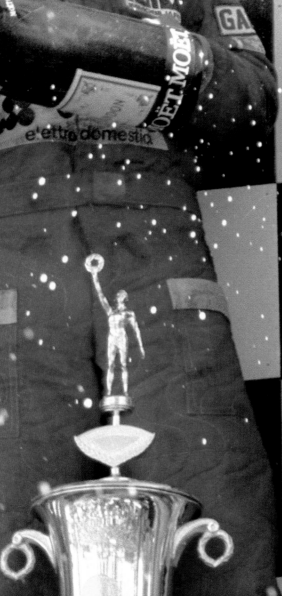

Felice Nazzaro (1881–1940)

Nazzaro, probably the greatest Italian driver of the period up to World War I, was apprenticed to the FIAT company at an early age, and was for some time employed as a chauffeur by Vincenzo Florio. He became a test engineer and then a racing driver for FIAT in the first years of this century, the company's formidable trio of drivers being made up by Vincenzo Lancia and Alessandro Cagno. Nazzaro's cool, immaculate style behind the wheel contrasted with the flashier brilliance of Lancia's; the latter sometimes drove faster than Nazzaro but in major events he often overtaxed his cars.

Nazzaro sprang to prominence in 1905 when he and Cagno took second and third places in the Gordon Bennett Cup in massive 75bhp FIATs; the following year, as we have seen in Chapter 4, he came second to Szisz in the first-ever *grand prix*. Nazzaro's greatest year, however, was 1907, when he won the three premier races of the season in three FIATs of quite different specification: the Targa Florio in the 7.4-litre 28-40hp '20-B' model; the Kaiserpreis (the German equivalent of a *grand prix*) in the 8-litre Taunus model; and the French Grand Prix with an F2, a massive 130hp, 16.3-litre racer capable of 177km/h (110mph). The following year Nazzaro came to

Brooklands in answer to a challenge by S. F. Edge, the promoter and driver of Napier racing cars. Nazzaro won in an immense Fiat SB-4 ('Mefisto'), which had an 18.2-litre engine developing no less than 175bhp. He also won the Coppa Florio at Bologna in 1908, and was now accepted as one of the great racing drivers of his day.

In 1911 Nazzaro (like Lancia three years before) left Fiat to set up in Turin as a manufacturer of high-performance cars. He won the Targa Florio in 1913 in one of his 4.5-litre models and the following year took the Coppa Florio for the second time. In 1916 he left the firm (Nazzaro cars continued in production until 1923, and Guido Meregalli won the 1920 Targa Florio in a pre-war model), and after the war he returned to Fiat as a racing driver. His crowning post-war achievement came in 1922 when, at the age of 41, he achieved victory in the French Grand Prix at Strasbourg in a 2-litre Fiat Tipo 804. These cars were remarkably fast for their day and capacity, but efforts to reduce their weight had made them dangerously fragile. (Nazzaro's pleasure in his outstanding victory was soured by the death in this race of his nephew Biaggio, in a similar Fiat, who was thrown onto the track when his 804's rear axle snapped.) He retired from racing after his car broke down in the Italian Grand Prix of 1924, but he remained on Fiat's staff until shortly before his death in 1940.

PRECEDING TWO PAGES Victors: breaking out the bubbly after the 1978 United States Grand Prix at Long Beach are winner Carlos Reutemann (Ferrari), with second-placed Mario Andretti (Lotus) on the right.

RIGHT INSET Felice Nazzaro, who was Fiat's number-one driver for more than 20 years.

BELOW Nazzaro's last major win was in the 1922 French Grand Prix at Strasbourg. Here he races ahead of the field in his Fiat Tipo 804. This was the first *grand prix* to feature a massed start.

BELOW RIGHT Nazzaro in the German Kaiserpreis (Emperor's Cup), one of his three major victories in the 1907 season.

E Morlant

N° 28

Georges Boillot (1885–1916)

During the Coupe de *L'Auto* of 1913, Georges Boillot was leading the race when he pulled into the pits, called for a glass of wine and – almost as an afterthought – inquired as to how his rivals were doing. Then, having stretched his legs, he climbed back into his car and drove to victory. The episode was typical of a man whose histrionic temperament, vanity, and outstanding brilliance as a driver made him the idol of the French public in the last years before World War I.

The Coupe de *L'Auto* was a race for cars with a capacity of up to 3 litres and it was often held in conjunction with the French Grand Prix in Edwardian days. Boillot was already famous by 1913, but he had earlier made his name as a development engineer and driver of small-capacity *voiturette* racers, notably with the bizarre Lion-Peugeot V-twin cars. Boillot remained faithful to the Peugeot marque throughout his racing career. One of the greatest achievements was his victory in the 1912 Grand Prix, which was held over two days at the Dieppe circuit. His conquest, in a 7.6-litre, 16-valve, double-overhead-camshaft Peugeot, of the Fiats of almost double the capacity driven by Louis Wagner and David Bruce-Brown heralded the demise of the huge, slow-revving *grand-prix* engines of earlier days. The following year he won not only the Coupe de *L'Auto* mentioned above but also the *grand prix* held at the same meeting at Amiens.

It was his heroic defeat in the 1914 *grand prix* at Lyons (see Chapter 4) that put the seal on his public fame – although in truth it was his impetuosity and his intense dislike of being led at any point in a race that enabled the German Mercedes team to cut him down on the closing laps. At the outbreak of World War I he joined the French air force, becoming one of the earliest fighter pilots in a unit known as *Les Sportifs*. In May 1916, in a spirit typical of his performance on the racetrack, he took on seven German scouts single-handed. The odds were hopeless, and Boillot died when his plane was shot out of the sky.

ABOVE Georges Boillot in one of his greatest victories, the French Grand Prix of 1912 at Dieppe. This was the last *grand prix* to be run over two days.

LEFT Boillot refuels his car while his mechanic changes a tyre during the 1912 race. In those days only the driver and his riding mechanic were allowed to do such work, or to carry out repairs, during the course of a *grand prix*.

Tazio Nuvolari (1892–1953)

'The Flying Mantuan' is still regarded by many as the greatest racing driver of all. At the height of his fame in the 1930s he was known simply but unequivocally as Il Maestro (The Master), and in Italy he was a national hero. On the racetrack his short, slight figure, clothed in a yellow turtle-neck sweater, blue trousers, and brown shoes with yellow laces, was instantly recognisable. At the wheel, his extraordinary facial contortions belied the cool, unspectacular economy of his driving style. He was possibly the inventor, and certainly the first complete master, of the technique of fast cornering known as the four-wheel drift.

He began his racing career on motor-cycles, rapidly establishing a reputation as a brilliant, if accident-prone, rider: he won more than 300 important events in Italy and abroad during the 1920s (he was Italian 500cc champion in 1924, riding British Nortons), and turned to motor-car racing in earnest only in 1927, when he took fifth place in the Mille Miglia.

His career in major sports-car races was concentrated mainly in the years 1930–5. During that period he won the Mille Miglia twice (1930, 1933) and was second once (1934); he won the Targa Florio twice (1931, 1932), the Le Mans 24-hours once (1933), and the RAC Tourist Trophy race twice (1930, 1933). He also won numerous hill-climb events in these years.

His greatest successes, however, were in *grands prix*. For most of the 1930s he was driving Alfa Romeos (and sometimes Maseratis) which from 1934 onwards were outclassed in specification and performance by the huge Mercedes-Benz and Auto Union racers. An idea of Nuvolari's genius can be seen in the fact that, between 1934 and 1936, he won 14 *grands prix* and was placed in nine others, while the great Rudolf Caracciola, the number one driver of the Mercedes-Benz team, won nine and was placed in four. His most famous victory was in the 1935 German Grand Prix (see Chapter 4). An almost equally startling demonstration of his skill came in the 1934 Monza Grand Prix. In order to lighten his Maserati for the weigh-in before the race, his crew drained the hydraulic fluid from the brake system – and then forgot to put it back! In spite of having virtually no brakes on this difficult circuit, Nuvolari came in fifth.

His courage was legendary. In 1934, with his right leg encased in plaster seven weeks after he had broken it in a crash at Alessandria, he entered for the Avus Grand Prix on the circuit near Berlin. Although he had only one usable foot to actuate the accelerator, clutch, and brake pedals, he took fourth place. He broke ribs so often that he had a special 'corset' of bandages made for him so that he could race while the fractures were mending.

Nuvolari was strenuously wooed by the managers of the Mercedes and Auto Union teams, and eventually he joined Auto Union in 1938, finishing fourth in his first race and winning the Italian and Donington *grands prix* that season – the latter after breaking a rib during a practice lap when a stag leapt in front of his car.

After World War II Nuvolari returned to racing for a few years, although by now he was suffering from a terminal respiratory illness. His two

greatest performances in this last, brief period were in the Mille Miglia of 1947 and 1948. The event was hardly ideal for an ailing man; moreover, in 1947 Nuvolari was driving an open Cisitalia of only 1.1 litres and had against him a team of 2.9-litre works Alfa Romeos led by Carlo Biondetti – the ace sports-car driver of the day. Although Biondetti could outpace him on the long straight stretches, Nuvolari showed all his old mastery in the mountains, with the result that at Bologna – with less than a quarter of the race to run – he was leading the race, nine minutes ahead of Biondetti. Then disaster struck on the road to Asti – the little Cisitalia ploughing to a halt in the middle of a huge, pond-deep puddle. By the time Nuvolari and his co-driver got the car working again, almost 20 minutes had been lost. Biondetti was far ahead and, moreover, was able to exploit the Alfa's performance to the full on the 240km (148-mile) *autostrada* on the last stage from Turin to Brescia. Even so Biondetti was only just over 15 minutes ahead of Nuvolari at the finish.

The following year the 56-year-old maestro persuaded Enzo Ferrari to let him have one of the new 2-litre Tipo 166s for the race. Biondetti was now Ferrari's number one sports-car driver and would be in the first-choice Tipo 166. This time it was the car's bodywork that let Nuvolari down. First the Ferrari bonnet came loose, flying over Nuvolari's head; later his driving seat came adrift. Finally, with the chassis weakening fast, the rear brakes ceased to function on the section between Bologna and Reggio, and Nuvolari was forced to retire. He was far in the lead at this time – Biondetti, the eventual winner, being more than half an hour behind.

Nuvolari had his last race in 1950 when, although 58 years of age and gravely ill, he drove a Cisitalia 1.5-litre to victory at the Monte Pellegrino circuit. At the end of the race he was almost unconscious and had to be lifted out of the car.

ABOVE Tazio Nuvolari in a 3-litre Auto Union D-type in the Swiss Grand Prix at Bremgarten in 1939. Joining the German team in 1938, Nuvolari quickly mastered the tricky handling of the mid-engined monster, which in 1939 was developing 485bhp with the aid of its two-stage supercharger.

BELOW The maestro, clad, as always, in a yellow sweater beneath a leather jacket. The greatest driver of the pre-war years, Nuvolari was supreme alike in *grand-prix* and sports-car racing.

Luigi Fagioli (1898–1952)

Fagioli's name springs less readily to mind than those of some of his Italian contemporaries, notably Nuvolari, Varzi, and Campari. But in the early 1930s he was one of the most highly regarded of *grand-prix* drivers. He took up racing in the mid-1920s, but first attracted wide attention in 1930, when he won three important races at the wheel of a Maserati. He drove for the Maserati team for three years, then joined Scuderia Ferrari, the organisation that was running the Alfa Romeo racing team. In 1933 he won three major events, including the Italian Grand Prix, for Alfa and was placed second in three others, and these successes were sufficient to make him champion of Italy that year.

At this time Mercedes-Benz was preparing the W25 model for what was to be an overwhelmingly successful *grand-prix* career, and its team manager, the great Alfred Neubauer, was looking for a driver to support Rudolf Caracciola. Thus it was that in 1934 Fagioli became the first major foreign driver to join one of the German works teams. Although Fagioli scored several important victories for Mercedes, including the Spanish, Italian,

and Monaco *grands prix*, his years with Neubauer were less than happy. The standard team instructions were that Caracciola, the number one driver, should win whenever possible. The tough, stocky, impetuous Italian rebelled against this discipline – understandably so, since his brilliant, if sometimes reckless, driving often made him quicker than the German. Fagioli and Caracciola began to quarrel – it is said they came to blows at least once – and in 1937 the Italian signed for the rival Auto Union team.

Fagioli retired the following year, but in 1950 he made a comeback with Alfa Romeo, forming a triumvirate of superb drivers with team-mates Giuseppe Farina and Juan Manuel Fangio – the famous 'Three Fs'. The Alfa Tipo 158 was almost unbeatable that year, and although Farina took the title and Fangio – until then little known in Europe – attracted most of the publicity, the 51-year-old Fagioli was placed in six of the major *grands prix*. that season. In 1951 he took the 1,100cc class in the Mille Miglia and the following year he was third overall. Then, while practising for the Monaco Grand Prix (an event for sports cars that season), he crashed in the Monte Carlo tunnel and died three weeks later from his injuries.

LEFT Luigi Fagioli making one of his celebrated fast starts aboard a Mercedes-Benz W25B in the 1935 Tripoli Grand Prix. His career with Mercedes was marred by team quarrels, but he often drove brilliantly for the German marque.

BELOW Fagioli after winning the International Race at the Avus circuit, near Berlin. in 1935 – a season in which the Mercedes-Benz team won nine of the 11 major races in which they were entered.

Rudolf Caracciola (1901–59)

In spite of his dark hair and Italian-sounding surname, Rudolf Caracciola was a German born in the Rhineland, the son of a hotelier of Remagen. He worked during the early 1920s for the Fafnir motor factory and drove the firm's 1.9-litre Type 471 sports car in his first race, at the Avus circuit, in 1922. His talent was soon spotted by Mercedes and he began his long career with the great Stuttgart firm in 1924, at first taking part mainly in hill-climb and sprint races. He was entered in the first-ever German Grand Prix, at the Avus in 1926, and leapt into immediate international prominence by winning the race, driving the ill-handling 2-litre Mercedes like a master on the rain-soaked track. He became European sports-car champion in 1930, and the following year he drove relentlessly to take the immensely powerful Mercedes-Benz SSKL to the first-ever non-Italian victory in the Mille Miglia.

In 1932, while the new generation of mighty Mercedes *grand-prix* racers was still in the design stage, he joined the Alfa Romeo team for a few races and found himself partnering Nuvolari. In the German Grand Prix that year – when the Italian maestro was almost unbeatable – Nuvolari's pit crew was ordered to 'go-slow' while changing his tyres and refuelling in order to allow Caracciola to achieve a popular local win. If this was a somewhat pyrrhic victory, Caracciola was to prove himself one of the great *grand-prix* drivers in the 1935–9 seasons. There is no doubt that the Mercedes-Benz and, to a lesser extent, the Auto Unions of that period were greatly in advance of anything the Italians or the French manufacturers could put against them. But equally the cars needed drivers of outstanding skill to get the best out of them, particularly the ferocious 5.7-litre, 646hp Mercedes-Benz W125 of 1936–7. Caracciola proved unquestionably the greatest of the team of Mercedes drivers of that era, winning no fewer than 14 *grands prix* (including the German race five times) in the last six seasons before World War II. He raced infrequently after the war, but in 1952 he delighted his many admirers by taking fourth place in the Mille Miglia.

Caracciola was involved in three major accidents. When practising in a private Alfa Romeo for the 1933 Monaco Grand Prix he crashed and broke his thigh – an injury that gave him a permanent limp and troubled him for many years. In 1946 he came out of retirement and, while practising for the Indianapolis 500 event in America, he was hit in the face by a bird. He was seriously concussed and unconscious for several days. Finally, his career was brought to an end in 1952 when, in a sports-car race, the brakes of his Mercedes-Benz 300SL 'gull-wing' coupé locked, the car crashed into a tree, and Caracciola's thigh fractured for the second time.

Note that only the last of these accidents occurred in an actual race (and that a sports-car event). Caracciola's touch on the *grand-prix* circuits was remarkably sensitive: he never overstrained his cars and rarely shredded his tyres. His immaculate driving occasionally gave rise to the claim that he was not so fast as other Mercedes and Auto Union drivers such as the flashier Bernd Rosemeyer and Manfred von Brauchitsch. His record effectively refutes that claim, and in technique he was far ahead of his German contemporaries until Hermann Lang began to rival him in the late 1930s. Moreover, Caracciola's skill in the wet was unrivalled in his day (he was known as *Regenmeister* – Rainmaster), and was probably unmatched in *grand-prix* racing until Stirling Moss reached his peak in the 1950s. Like other Mercedes and Auto Union drivers, Caracciola also competed in major hill-climb events in the 1930s. Although not so great in this field as *Bergmeister* Hans Stuck, he broke the record for the exceptionally difficult Klausen hill-climb in a Mercedes W25 in 1934.

Rudolf Caracciola (inset) was the greatest of the German drivers of the 1930s and the one most suited by temperament and skill to get the best out of the formidable Mercedes-Benz racers of the period. The crowning achievement of the marque in those days was the W154 of 1938 and its very similar successor, the W163 of 1939. In the main picture above, Caracciola pilots the W154 in the 1938 French Grand Prix at Rheims, where he came second to his team-mate Manfred von Brauchitsch.

Achille Varzi (1904–48)

Varzi was a lifelong friend and rival of Nuvolari, and like him first made a reputation racing motorcycles. Their professional association began in 1927 when they and their two brilliant mechanics, Decimo Campagnoni and Guido Bignami, formed the Italian Bugatti team, which achieved a remarkable record of successes in its first season. The following year, however, Varzi bought an aging Alfa Romeo P2 *grand-prix* car from Giuseppe Campari and drove it into second place in the European Grand Prix at Monza. His brilliant performance resulted in Varzi joining the Alfa works team in 1929, and the following year he won the Italian championship and also the Targa Florio. By now Nuvolari was also in the Alfa team, and in 1931 Varzi left to drive Maseratis and Bugattis, sharing a Bugatti Type 51 with Louis Chiron to win the French Grand Prix.

Varzi's rivalry with Nuvolari during this period is legendary. Two of their greatest tussles were in the Monaco Grand Prix of 1932 and 1933, the narrow, serpentine streets of the circuit drawing out all the flair and technical virtuosity of both drivers. In the 1932 race the two exchanged the lead almost continuously for 50 laps until Varzi's Bugatti suffered engine failure. The following year the rivals staged an even more exhilarating sequel, racing nose to tail, far ahead of the rest of the field and at lap speeds that most experts had thought impossible on this circuit. On the final, 100th lap, it looked as if motor-racing history might see the first-ever dead-heat, but a few hundred metres before the finish line Varzi at last forced his way in front, and Nuvolari's engine caught fire as he made a desperate effort to respond. In 1934 Varzi rejoined Alfa, whose team was now managed by Enzo Ferrari. Racing in the superb 2.6-litre P3 Monoposto (single-seat) *grand-prix* car, Varzi won seven of the major races that season and also brilliantly won the Mille Miglia and Targa Florio in Alfa 6C-2300s against powerful challenges from Nuvolari, Louis Chiron, and others.

Varzi became the second great Italian driver (after Fagioli) to join one of the resurgent German *grand-prix* works teams, signing for Auto Union in 1935. Although he had mixed fortunes with this marque, his outstanding talent enabled him to adapt quickly to the unusual handling of the rear-engined monster. In 1936, however, a violent gust of wind blew his car off the straight in the Tripoli Grand Prix when he was travelling at over 260km/h (161mph). Varzi miraculously emerged unhurt from the crash, but the incident affected him profoundly (it was his first crash of any consequence) and he never seemed to regain his former virtuosity. He later became addicted to cocaine and went into semi-retirement before World War II.

He made a post-war *grand-prix* comeback with the 1946 Alfa Romeo team, driving the superb 1.5-litre, straight-eight Tipo 158 'Alfetta' that had been designed by Gioacchino Colombo before the war. He won two important races at Turin and Bari and was placed second in the Buenos Aires, Swiss, Belgian, and Italian *grands prix*. In 1948, when practising for the Swiss Grand Prix at Bremgarten, his car got into an uncontrollable skid on the rain-soaked track, overturned, and Varzi was crushed to death.

In temperament and appearance Varzi was the opposite of Nuvolari – impeccably dressed, phlegmatic and undemonstrative at the wheel; cool and introspective in company. Like Nuvolari, he was a great all-rounder. As a *grand-prix* driver only Nuvolari and perhaps Rudolf Caracciola bettered him in the early 1930s; as a sports-car driver during this period he was the peer of Nuvolari and Giuseppe Campari.

ABOVE RIGHT Varzi at a meeting in Parma in 1934.

RIGHT Varzi (Bugatti Type 51) takes the tightest line through Station hairpin during his epic duel with Nuvolari (Alfa Romeo) in the 1932 Monaco Grand Prix – probably the greatest race ever seen on the circuit.

Juan Manuel Fangio (born 1911)

If Nuvolari has a rival as the greatest *grand-prix* driver of all time, most people's choice would be the taciturn Argentinian, Juan Manuel Fangio. Stirling Moss, second driver to Fangio in the all-conquering Mercedes-Benz *grand-prix* team of 1955, regarded El Chueco ('Bandy Legs') as the best he had ever seen, asserting that his finest racing education was to drive a couple of lengths behind the Argentinian maestro in a *grand prix*.

He began his racing career in 1934 running souped-up Model A Fords in long-distance road races. His first major success, at the age of 29, was in a kind of Argentinian combination of the Safari Rally and the Mille Miglia – the 1940 Gran Premio Internacional del Norte, a 9,530km (5,920-mile) race in 13 stages from Buenos Aires to Lima (Peru) and back. He won in a Chevrolet coupé 'special'. Wartime restrictions put an end to racing, but in 1948 he was invited to drive a 1.5-litre Maserati 4CL *grand-prix* car in the annual race series at Buenos Aires. A number of top European drivers were participating, including Achille Varzi, Alberto Ascari, Luigi Villoresi, and Jean-Pierre Wimille (that year perhaps the greatest driver in the world). Varzi befriended Fangio and gave him valuable advice on how to drive *grand-prix* thoroughbreds. The following year he won the Mar del Plata Grand Prix, and then left for Europe to head a team of Argentinian Maseratis, taking over Varzi's racing workshop.

In view of Fangio's astounding record, it is worth remembering that he began his assault on the world championships when he was 38 – an age when most drivers are thinking of retiring. He won his first European race, the San Remo Grand Prix, and went on to a string of further victories in the 1949 season. He was then invited to join the Alfa Romeo Tipo 158 team for 1950. He had a remarkable season, winning the Belgian, French, and Moroccan *grands prix* and coming a close second in the world championship to his teammate, Dr Giuseppe ('Nino') Farina. The following year he achieved his ambition, winning the drivers' title in the Tipo 159, now getting 420bhp from its supercharged 1.5-litre engine.

In 1952 Fangio suffered the only major injury of his career, in a 2-litre race at Monza. Bad weather had grounded flights from France, and Fangio was obliged to drive the 800km (500 miles) from Paris to Milan. He arrived, exhausted, only two hours before the race, and had no chance to put in any practice run. On the second lap of the race he accelerated too soon out of a corner, the car somersaulted, and Fangio was flung out and broke his neck. He raced no more that season.

In 1954 he started with Maserati (winning two *grands prix*) but was then lured away to Mercedes-Benz, which had now launched its superlative fuel-injected 2.5-litre, straight-eight W196. The car and the driver were each superior to any other contenders; together they waltzed away with the world championships, and they repeated the feat in 1955. Fangio moved to Ferrari the following year (Mercedes-Benz having withdrawn from racing), and won his fourth title in Ferrari racers that were, in fact, Lancia D50 V8 cars, designed by the great, if now venerable, Vittorio Jano.

Fangio's fifth title – and fourth in a row – came in 1957, when in a Maserati 250F, a 2.5-litre straight-six, he won the Argentine, Monaco, French, and German *grands prix*. (This car, the finest racer Maserati ever made, was already quite a veteran – Fangio having driven one to victory in its first-ever *grand prix* in 1954.) The maestro retired the following year.

Fangio's reputation rests not only on his 24 championship-qualifying victories in four different makes of car, nor even on the cool perfection of his technique. He had the gift, unmatched in his time, of being able to nurse sick cars to victory; his determination was matched by his patience, and he always drove only as fast as was absolutely necessary. That he could also drive with unparalleled ferocity was shown in the title-clinching German Grand Prix of 1957, when he broke the lap record five times in the first 11 laps (improving his own 1956 figure by more than 12 seconds); lost over a minute in a disastrously slow refuelling stop; set off in pursuit of Mike Hawthorn and Peter Collins in the immensely fast Lancia-Ferraris; and finally destroyed the hopes of the British drivers on the 20th lap, when he sliced a further six seconds off an already astonishing lap record. It is against performances like this that the claims to greatness of other post-war drivers have to be measured: in his own day Fangio was peerless.

ABOVE Juan Manuel Fangio, the greatest post-war *grand-prix* driver, on his way to perhaps his most astonishing victory – the German Grand Prix of 1957, in which he broke the lap record no fewer than 10 times in his Maserati 250F. Fangio took his fifth drivers' title that year at the age of 46, and retired the following season. His career ratio of 24 *grand-prix* victories in 51 starts remains unapproached.

BELOW Fangio photographed at a race meeting in 1976.

Alberto Ascari (1918–55)

'Ciccio' Ascari was the son of Antonio Ascari, the most famous Italian driver of the early 1920s. The young Alberto found a gifted mentor in Luigi Villoresi, who encouraged him to begin his racing career on motor-cycles, as Nuvolari and Varzi had done. Ascari drove in his first important motor-car race in 1940, when Enzo Ferrari offered him a drive in his very first model, the Tipo 815, in the shortened Mille Miglia of that year. After the war he drove Cisitalias for a while, and his performances brought him an invitation to drive for the Maserati works team. Here he again came under the guidance of Villoresi, and he won an important victory at Modena in one of the new Maserati A6Gs in 1947.

By 1949, when Villoresi and Ascari joined Ferrari, it was evident that the pupil was a faster driver than his mentor, and Ascari won the Italian and Swiss *grands prix* in supercharged 1.5-litre Ferrari Tipo 166s. Alfa Romeo dominated the championship the following year, but Ascari proved unbeatable in Formula 2 events, and in 1951 he helped to break Alfa's *grand-prix* monopoly by winning the Spanish and Italian events in the unblown 4.5-litre Tipo 375 designed by Aurelio Lampredi, Ferrari's new chief engineer.

Ascari's two greatest seasons were 1952 and 1953, when the championship was run to Formula 2 rules – 2-litre, unsupercharged cars. It was an unexciting formula, but Lampredi came up with a car supremely well suited to its purpose, the four-cylinder Tipo 500. For two years Ascari proved virtually unbeatable except on the rare occasions when his car suffered mechanical failure: he won 11 of the 14 qualifying *grands prix* in which he took part, and in both seasons won the drivers' title by a huge margin.

In 1954 Ascari and Villoresi were persuaded to join Lancia: the formula had changed to 2.5 litres and the famous Italian marque (for long out of *grand-prix* racing) was preparing its formidable D50 V8s. The cars took a long time to develop, and Ascari spent the season driving other marques – although he won the Mille Miglia in the splendid 3.3-litre Lancia D24 sports car. The following season the D50s were introduced, proving tremendously fast if difficult to handle. In the Monaco Grand Prix Ascari was leading on the 80th lap when he came out of the tunnel. He braked to negotiate the chicane on the waterfront, one of his front wheels locked, and the Lancia plunged into the waters of the harbour. Amazingly, Ascari escaped with bruises; but he was severely shaken, and four days later at Monza he borrowed a 3-litre Ferrari sports car to test his nerve. On his third lap the car struck the edge of the track and rolled over. Ascari was rescued from the wreck but died soon afterwards, before he could be got to hospital. Like his father, he was killed at the age of 36 on the 26th day of the month.

MAIN PICTURE Alberto Ascari corners in his Lancia D50 in the 1955 Monaco race. Shortly after, his brakes locked and the car dived into the harbour.

INSET Ascari after winning the British Grand Prix at Silverstone in 1953, the year in which he took his second drivers' title in the Ferrari Tipo 500.

Sir Jack Brabham (born 1926)

'Black Jack' Brabham is the oldest and perhaps the most gifted of the many Australians and New Zealanders who have made their mark in post-war *grand-prix* racing. He arrived in Britain in 1955, having gained valuable experience driving a Cooper-Bristol in his native New South Wales and New Zealand, and that year he made his debut in the British Grand Prix at Aintree in a mid-engined Cooper. During the next three seasons Brabham drove exclusively for Cooper (apart from a brief, unsuccessful foray with a Maserati 250F in 1956); he proved a formidable competitor in Formula 2 events, taking the championship in 1958.

In 1959 Cooper entered its Coventry-Climax-engined 2.5-litre cars in Formula 1 events, and they just managed to beat Ferrari – Brabham taking the title in the United States Grand Prix at Sebring, when he had to push his fuel-less car over the finishing line. He repeated his title win the following year, but this time his success was utterly decisive, for he took no fewer than five

grandes épreuves in succession; the mid-engined *grand-prix* car was here to stay.

By the end of the 1961 season the Coopers had proved too slow in the new 1.5-litre formula. Brabham now decided to branch out on his own as a driver and constructor, and for 1963 he signed the American Dan Gurney as second driver. The new team won its first championship event the following year, Gurney and Brabham coming in first and third in the French Grand Prix. The New Zealander Denny Hulme joined the team for 1965, but it proved an unsuccessful season and Gurney left at the end of the year.

In 1966 the hurriedly introduced 3-litre formula caught most of the constructors napping – except for Brabham, who soon had an Australian Repco engine in highly competitive trim. The simple, not very powerful, but utterly reliable engine, combined with the excellent handling and balance of the chassis designed by Brabham himself, proved the best of the bunch that season. Brabham himself won the French, British, Dutch, and German *grands prix*, taking the drivers' title and becom-

ing the first driver in history to take the constructors' title in a car of his own design; he was also the first driver after Fangio to take the title three times. (The season was, in fact, Brabham's finest, for Honda-powered Brabhams virtually swept the board in Formula 2.) In 1967 Denny Hulme took the drivers' title and won the constructors' title for Repco-Brabham, while Brabham himself was runner-up.

Brabham retired after the 1970 season, selling up his business and returning to Australia. As a driver he was the most ruthlessly determined of his day; he had an iron-hard will to win, but he also had the sense and ability to persuade a basically inferior car into second or third place when victory was out of the question. As a designer, his driving experience and his qualifications in engineering enabled him to break new ground. In particular, he was a pioneer in the art of chassis-tuning – that is, modifying the suspension and braking systems of a car to suit the characteristics of a particular circuit. He was knighted in 1979 for his services to motor sport.

LEFT Jack-Brabham, who won the drivers' title three times, was an unsparing competitor: drivers pursuing him in faster machinery sometimes accused him of having the widest car in the business. But his gifts as a driver-designer-constructor are unique in *grand-prix* history.

BELOW Brabham on his way to victory in the British Grand Prix at Brands Hatch in 1966. This was the first year of the 3-litre formula, and Brabham took his third drivers' title as well as the constructors' title in his Repco-Brabham.

John Michael Hawthorn (1929–58)

Mike Hawthorn was the son of a well-known engine tuner, and it was almost inevitable that he would enter motor sport. His first race was in 1950, when he and his father competed in the Brighton Speed Trials in Riley two-seaters. The following year he won the Ulster and Leinster trophies in Ireland and also competed successfully in several meetings at Goodwood. It was in 1952 that he broke through to national prominence in a 2-litre Cooper-Bristol, winning his first two races at the Goodwood Easter meeting and chasing home Froilan Gonzalez's 4.5-litre Thinwall Special in the Richmond Trophy – all on the same day! He quickly graduated to *grand-prix* racing that season, taking fourth place in his first event at Spa. By now he was attracting international attention, and he accepted an invitation to drive for Ferrari in 1953. He crowned his first season for the Italian team by beating the great Fangio by a whisker in the French Grand Prix. It was an historic occasion, for Hawthorn had become the first British driver to win a championship event since the young Richard Seaman (Mercedes-Benz) won the German Grand Prix in 1938.

At the beginning of the 1954 season his car crashed in flames in a race at Syracuse and he was severely burnt about the legs. After driving briefly for the not-yet-competitive British Vanwall, he returned to Ferrari in 1955 but had little success. That year he drove a Jaguar D-Type at Le Mans and he and Ivor Bueb won after Mercedes-Benz withdrew its 300SLRs following Pierre Levegh's appalling crash. Hawthorn spent 1956 with the unsuccessful BRM team, once again returning to Ferrari for 1957 and coming fourth in the drivers' championship. The next season was his best, and he took the title by virtue of one victory and five second places (Moss, who won four *grandes épreuves*, was only one point behind him.) That year, too, saw the death of his team-mate Luigi Musso and of his closest friend, Peter Collins, and at the end of the season Hawthorn announced his retirement.

Hawthorn won only three *grandes épreuves* in his six professional seasons. He was a temperamental driver, in the sense that he would drive with absolute brilliance when the mood took him but could perform listlessly on other occasions. He achieved enormous popularity at a time when the British racing public's idea of a hero was a handsome, beer-drinking, practical-joking young man who seemed to embody the old tradition of the romantic amateur. Hawthorn was much more than this – and he was, moreover, Britain's first-ever world-champion driver. But he seems to have been living up to his public image on that morning in January 1959 when he drove at reckless speed down the Hog's Back, near Guildford. He lost control on a patch of wet road, wrapped his Jaguar around a tree, and died instantly.

Stirling Moss (born 1929)

Moss was born into a motor-sport family, his father having raced in the 1920s and 1930s and his mother having been a talented trials and rally driver (his sister Pat, who married Erik Carlsson, was undoubtedly the best woman rally driver of her time). Moss began his career in 1948 in Formula 3 and hill-climb events, mainly in the tiny but very fast rear-engined Cooper 500cc racers. His exceptional talent was quickly appreciated and he soon moved on to *voiturette* events with the HWM team, and to saloon-car racing (in which he had a string of victories in Jaguars in the British championship events).

His first championship-qualifying event was the Swiss Grand Prix of 1951 at Berne in an HWM, but his problem during the next few years was to find a British *grand-prix* car that would do justice to his talent. (Mike Hawthorn, in contrast, was quick to answer an invitation from Enzo Ferrari, and so tasted *grand-prix* fame much earlier than Moss.) In 1954 Moss bowed to the inevitable and bought a Maserati 250F to campaign in *grands prix*, taking third place in his first race (the Belgian Grand Prix) and almost at once securing a place in the Maserati works team. In the Italian Grand Prix at Monza that year Moss drove brilliantly, outpacing the very fast Mercedes-Benz W196s of Fangio and Lang until, with only 10 laps to go, his petrol tank developed a leak and ran out of fuel. His performance, however, secured him a place in the Mercedes-Benz team in 1955 as second driver to Fangio. At the end of 1955 Mercedes withdrew from all racing and Moss returned to Maserati for 1956, winning the Monaco and Italian *grands prix* and many non-qualifying races. For 1957 and 1958 he drove for Vanwall – the first British marque to have a realistic chance of winning the world championship. During 1957 he and Tony Brooks won the British Grand Prix at Aintree, and Moss went on to take a Vanwall to victory in the Italian Grand Prix. The following year he won the Dutch, Portuguese, and Moroccan *grands prix*; and then he achieved one of his greatest victories, the Argentine Grand Prix, in a prototype mid-engined Cooper powered by a Coventry-Climax engine.

In 1960 Moss drove one of the fast but fragile new lightweight Lotus 18s, winning the Monaco Grand Prix, but then he suffered serious injury (including fractures of both legs) when the car lost a rear wheel during practice for the Belgian Grand Prix. Remarkably, his injuries caused Moss to miss only two *grands prix*, and he went on to win the United States Grand Prix later in the season. For 1961, with the new 1.5-litre formula in force, Moss continued to campaign with the now-obsolescent Lotus 18, winning the Monaco and German *grands prix* against all odds; he also drove the Ferguson four-wheel drive car to its sole Formula 1 victory, a non-qualifying event at Oulton Park. His racing career came to an end the following year when his Lotus 18/21 crashed inexplicably during a race at the Goodwood Easter Meeting and Moss suffered serious brain injuries.

Moss never won the world drivers' championship, but he is without question the finest driver never to do so, and his expertise in the wet rivalled Caracciola's. He was the runner-up for four years running (1955–8) and came third for the next three (1959–61). If there is some doubt as to whether he, Jim Clark, or Jackie Stewart was the greatest British *grand-prix* driver of all time, there can be no argument that he was the finest all-rounder produced by any country since World War II. His enormous talent for sports-car racing – comparable, among the greatest *grand-prix* drivers, only to Nuvolari and Varzi – reached its peak in 1955 when he won the Mille Miglia, Targa Florio, and Tourist Trophy in a Mercedes-Benz 300SLR, securing the championship for Mercedes; and he was a key figure in the championship-winning Jaguars and Aston Martins during the late-1950s. He was also supreme as a rally driver, and was one of only two drivers ever to win the greatly coveted Coupe des Alpes en Or for unpenalised runs three years in succession in the Alpine Rally.

ABOVE Stirling Moss, oil- and dust-stained after his superb victory in the 1955 Mille Miglia. Without question the finest European all-rounder since the war, Moss excelled alike in *grands prix*, sports-car races, and rallies.

BELOW Moss aboard one of his favourite cars, the Maserati 250F, in the 1956 Monaco Grand Prix, which he led from start to finish – the first of his three victories in six years in this event.

Graham Hill (1929–75)

Graham Hill was an attractive anomaly in *grand-prix* racing. Unlike Hawthorn and Moss – his exact contemporaries – he had no advantage of wealth or family interest to help his entry into racing; unlike Clark, Stewart, and many others he does not seem to have been born with a 'natural' flair for driving. He reached the top by enormous determination, hard graft, and a remarkable capacity to learn from his own and others' errors. After working as a driver-mechanic for several seasons he joined Lotus as a driver in 1958, but lack of success in the notoriously fragile Lotus 12s led to his joining the crisis-torn BRM team the following year. He remained faithful to BRM for six seasons, his patience being rewarded by BRM's only championship, and Hill's first world title, in 1962. For the next three years he was runner-up for the drivers' title, his great rival during this period being Jim Clark. In 1966 Hill won bravely, if somewhat fortuitously, the Indianapolis 500 race (and a considerable fortune) in a Lola-Ford.

The following year he teamed up with Clark to drive the Lotus 49s powered by the Ford Cosworth 3-litre V8 in *grands prix*; both of them, Hill especially, had an indifferent season, but in 1968 the car's reliability was transformed and Hill went on to take the drivers' title in the last *grand prix* of the season. The year 1969 saw him win the Monaco Grand Prix for a record fifth time, but a terrible accident, due to a faulty tyre, almost cost him his life in the United States Grand Prix at Watkins Glen. He was permanently crippled and never regained his form as a *grand-prix* driver; but in 1972 he surprised and delighted the motor-racing world by winning, with Henri Pescarolo, the Le Mans 24-hour race in a Matra-Simca.

From 1973 onwards he raced his own Cosworth-powered Shadow and Lola *grand-prix* cars, 1975 employing Allan Jones and Tony Brise as his top drivers and doing little racing himself. In November of that year, when returning from testing a new car on the Ricard-Castellet circuit, the aircraft Hill was piloting crashed on the northern outskirts of London; Hill, Tony Brise, the team manager, the team designer, and two others were killed.

Hill was perhaps the most popular British driver of the 1960s – the public responding alike to his remarkable self-made success in racing and to his talent as an after-dinner speaker. If he was not the greatest driver of his day, his combination of *grand-prix* drivers' titles and victories in the Indy 500 and Le Mans 24-hour race remains a unique treble in motor-sport annals.

Graham Hill (BRM) on his way to the first of his record-breaking five victories in the Monaco Grand Prix in 1963. The picture captures well the flavour of this event, which takes in many of the most famous thoroughfares in Monte Carlo. Hill's great popularity in Britain rested at least partly on his loyalty to the long-unsuccessful BRM. The car finally came good in 1962, when Hill took it to four championship wins and the drivers' title. The BRM was unique among British *grand-prix* cars of its time in using the marque's own, rather than proprietary, engine and transmission.

Jim Clark (1937–68)

Clark, the son of a Scottish gentleman farmer, began his sporting career in local sprints and went on to compete successfully in sports-car events in the 1950s. His all-too-brief *grand-prix* life was launched in 1961 when he became the top driver for Lotus (he had been driving Lotus Formula 2 cars since the year before). He was to drive Lotus cars for the rest of his career. His immense talent and his affinity for Colin Chapman's cars became sensationally apparent in December 1961 when he won the South African, the Natal, and the Rand *grands prix* in the space of 17 days. The next year Graham Hill beat him to the drivers' title by a whisker after Clark had won the *grands prix* of Belgium, Britain, United States, and Mexico. In 1963, however, Clark was virtually unbeatable in the wonderful Lotus 25. It was, indeed, a miraculous year: he scored a record seven *grand-épreuve* victories and wrapped up the title while there were three qualifying events still to be run. He also took second place at Indianapolis in a mid-engined Lotus-Ford which the old hands at the famous 'Brickyard' had dismissed as little better than a toy. In 1965 he regained the title – and at Indianapolis he went one better, leading for all but 10 of the 200 laps and becoming the first European driver to win the 500 for 45 years. For 1966, the first year of the 3-litre formula, Clark had to make do with the 2-litre Lotus while the team's 3-litre engines were being prepared. The following year the Brabham racers, with their well-tried Repco engines, prevailed, although Clark pressed Denny Hulme and Jack Brabham for the title, winning his fifth British Grand Prix and his third United States and Mexican.

By 1968 Colin Chapman had got the bugs out of what was to prove an all-conquering car – the Lotus 49 powered by the remarkable Cosworth V8 engine – and the racing world anticipated an almost inevitable third title for Clark. In April that year, however, he was racing a Lotus 48 Formula 2 car at Hockenheim, West Germany, when for reasons still unknown the car skidded off the circuit and crashed broadside into a tree; Clark died in hospital shortly afterwards.

Clark is regarded by many as the greatest *grand-prix* driver since Fangio. He shared Fangio's remarkably cool, economical driving style, his ability to nurse an ailing car to victory, and (apart from the mysterious Hockenheim crash) his comparative freedom from serious injury. His record speaks for itself: he won 25 of the 72 *grands prix* he entered – a ratio bettered only by Fangio's astonishing 24 victories out of 51. Also like Fangio, Clark was inferior to Moss as an all-rounder: although he appeared often in a variety of British saloon-car and other races, he never took part in the classic sports-car endurance races (in particular, he shared Colin Chapman's intense distaste for the Le Mans 24-hour event). But on the grand-prix circuits Clark was the undisputed master of his time.

Jim Clark was perhaps the finest-ever British *grand-prix* driver, his ratio of wins to starts being bettered only by the great Fangio's. His championship career was spent entirely with Lotus. The painting shows him in process of winning the famous Indianapolis 500 race in 1965. For this event his Lotus was powered by an American Ford 4.2-litre, four-cam V8 engine running on alcohol. The body of the car was offset slightly to the left to improve handling on the all-left-hand turns of the circuit.

Jackie Stewart (born 1939)

Stewart can be seen in retrospect as Clark's natural heir to *grand-prix* honours. Like Clark he was a small, slight (though much less taciturn) Scotsman born into a prosperous family. His older brother Jimmy was a driver before him, working for the successful Écurie Écosse outfit in the 1950s. At this time Jackie was an Olympics-standard clay-pigeon shot – a sport demanding the sort of reflexes and hand-eye co-ordination he was later to display on the circuits.

Stewart's serious entry to motor racing came in 1963 after Ken Tyrell had offered him a test drive in a Formula 3 Cooper-BMC at Goodwood. His rise through Formula 3 and Formula 2 was sensational. In 1964 he won all but two of the Formula 3 races he entered; finished second in his very first Formula 2 race; and in December, while deputising for Jim Clark, he won the second heat of the Formula 1 Rand Grand Prix in South Africa. He instantly became the hottest property among the *grand-prix* 'rookies', and joined BRM as second driver to Graham Hill for the 1965 season. He won the Italian Grand Prix, was second in the Belgian and Dutch, third at Monaco – and took third place in the drivers' championship behind Clark and Hill.

What promised to be a meteoric rise to the top was interrupted in 1966 when, on a rain-flooded Spa circuit in the Belgian Grand Prix, Stewart's BRM spun off the track. He was rescued by Graham Hill – whose BRM had also crashed – who helped to cut him free from the wrecked car. Stewart had a broken shoulder and a cracked rib.

For 1968, with the BRM in decline, Stewart re-joined Ken Tyrell (for whom he had continued to race Formula 2 cars in 1965–7). Tyrell was now fitting his Matra cars with the Cosworth V8 engine hitherto available only to Lotus. In this first season

the Matra-Ford proved fast but not always reliable; Stewart, in addition, broke his wrist in a Formula 2 race at Jarama (Spain) and had to miss a couple of championship-qualifying races. But he won the Dutch Grand Prix at Zandfoort, and followed this by one of his supreme performances, winning the German Grand Prix at the rain- and fog-blanketed Nürburgring by the almost ridiculous margin of four minutes. In spite of his injury, Stewart was runner up to Graham Hill for the driver's title.

The following year the Matra-Ford was almost invincible, Stewart taking the title with six victories. For 1970 Tyrell used March bodies (Matra using theirs to clothe a new V12 engine of their own design) and Stewart won only a single *grand prix*. But in 1971, after early-season failures, Stewart clinched his second title with victories in the Spanish, Monaco, French, British, German, and Canadian *grands prix* – his win on the tortuous Monaco circuit being achieved without benefit of rear-wheel brakes! Stewart's third and last title came in 1973 – his fourth place at Monza, after a supremely determined effort following a lengthy pit stop, giving him enough points to frustrate Emerson Fittipaldi's challenge for Lotus.

Stewart's total of 27 *grandes épreuves* (out of 99 starts) may never be surpassed now that drivers are retiring at a relatively early age. Like Fangio and Clark before him (and like Niki Lauda in 1975–7) he dominated most of the races he entered so long as his car was up to scratch. Stewart was an heir to the Jack Brabham tradition of technologist drivers. He spent countless hours testing the suspension systems and tyres of his cars and contributed significantly to the art of 'setting-up' racers for specific circuits. Both before and since his retirement he has been a powerful influence in the cause of safety in all forms of racing.

ABOVE One of Jackie Stewart's greatest triumphs was in the German Grand Prix in 1968 at the Nürburgring. On this notoriously difficult circuit and in mist and rain, his four-minute victory margin reflected Stewart's total mastery of his rivals.

BELOW Stewart, seen here in his heyday with Tyrell, won a record-breaking 27 *grandes épreuves* and three world drivers' titles in his nine-year Formula 1 career.

Index

Acknowledgements

The publishers thank the following for their kind permission to reproduce the pictures in this book:

Autocar 48 below left; Bentley Drivers Club 49 above right; Mercedes-Benz 7 above right, 59 above; Hugh Bishop 10–11, 21 below left, 22, 23, 27, 33, 34–35; Diana Burnett 2–3; Mary Evans Picture Library 6; Ford 32 below; Geoffrey Goddard Collection 1, 7 below right, 8 above right, 20 above, 38, 39, 40 below right, 41, 42–43 below, 48 above right, 51, 56, 61 below, 67, 68–69, 70–71 below, 73, 74 above and below left, 78, 79 and inset, 80 above right and below left, 81 above and below right, 83 above and inset, 85 below right, 88–89, 90 inset; Georges Ham (photo: Geoffrey Goddard) 48 above right, 49 above left, 57; Keystone Press Agency 32 above left; LAT 14–15, 16–17, 24, 26 above and below, 28, 30 above and below right, 34 below, 50 above and below right, 51 inset, 52–53, 64, 66, 71 above, 72, 76–77, 85 above, 86–87, 89 inset, 90, 91, 92–93, 94 below right, 95 above and below right; National Motor Museum 8 below right, 9 above, 61 above; Peugeot 59 below right; Popperfoto 87 inset; Cyril Posthumus 9 below, 12, 40 above, 45, 62, 82 below left and right; Pubbli Aer Photo 20 below; Peter Roberts Collection 60 above right and below left; Nigel Snowdon endpaper, 4–5, 29, 36–37, 42–43 above, 54–55, 74–75; Thirlby Collection 19, 21 above right; Michael Turner 46–47, 63, 64–65, 94 below left; Franco Zagari 18 above right and below left, 44 above right and below, 84 above and below right.